T0067130

JIMMY CARTER

With Family, Friends and Foes

MICHAEL SPENCER HAYES

authorHOUSE®

AuthorHouse™
1663 Liberty Drive
Bloomington, IN 47403
www.authorhouse.com
Phone: 1 (800) 839-8640

© *2015 Michael Spencer Hayes. All rights reserved.*

No part of this book may be reproduced, stored in a retrieval system, or transmitted by any means without the written permission of the author.

Published by AuthorHouse 04/24/2015

ISBN: 978-1-5049-0887-0 (sc)
ISBN: 978-1-5049-0888-7 (e)

Print information available on the last page.

Any people depicted in stock imagery provided by Thinkstock are models, and such images are being used for illustrative purposes only. Certain stock imagery © Thinkstock.

This book is printed on acid-free paper.

Because of the dynamic nature of the Internet, any web addresses or links contained in this book may have changed since publication and may no longer be valid. The views expressed in this work are solely those of the author and do not necessarily reflect the views of the publisher, and the publisher hereby disclaims any responsibility for them.

NASB
Scripture quotations marked NASB are taken from the New American Standard Bible®, Copyright © 1960, 1962, 1963, 1968, 1971, 1972, 1973, 1975, 1977, 1995 by The Lockman Foundation. Used by permission.

CONTENTS

INTRODUCTION: SAINT PATRICK'S DAY xi

I   LASTING IMPRESSIONS 1

II   STRIVING FOR APPROVAL 9

III   FILLING THE LARGEST OF SHOES 15

IV   FIRST STEPS ON THE ROAD TO HISTORY 25

V   THE PRODIGAL SON 34

VI   DETERMINATION 40

VII   ENOUGH ADVENTURE FOR A LIFETIME 50

VIII THY SEA IS SO GREAT 69

IX   A "CHAINSAW" FOR CHRISTMAS 79

X   "MY FRIEND JIMMY" 87

XI   A NATIONAL JOKE 94

XII   CRISIS AND LOSS 100

XIII BILLYGATE 110

XIV "MIZ LILLIAN, WHERE ARE
       YOU GOING NEXT?" 116

XV   AN ACTIVIST IN THE FAMILY 121

XVI A SECOND CHANCE 127

AFTERWORD 135

EPILOGUE: FINISHING STRONG 141

**DEDICATED TO THE PEOPLE OF
PLAINS, GEORGIA**

ACKNOWLEDGEMENTS

I am exceedingly grateful to Dr. Franklin C. Cacciutto for giving of his valuable time to proofread and edit this book. I would also like to thank Dr. Steve Hochman of the Carter Center, who has been very generous with his advice. Thanks to Governor Cecil Andrus, of Idaho, who served President Carter as Secretary of the Interior, for talking to me about Carter's contributions to the environment. I want to express my appreciation to Dr. Richard Harmond for his early support and encouragement. Also, thank you to Bill Lane for his valuable insights. Thank you Laura Tanner, Allene Haugabook, C. L. Walters and Jan Williams for sharing your knowledge of Plains and of President Carter with me. Many thanks to my wife, Nora Hayes, for listening to my ideas and patiently supporting me throughout the creation of this work.

SAINT PATRICK'S DAY

"**I believe that anyone can be successful in life, regardless of natural talent or the environment within which we live. This is not based on measuring success by human competitiveness for wealth, possessions, influence, and fame, but adhering to God's standards of truth, justice, humility, service, compassion, forgiveness, and love.**" **- Jimmy Carter (Humanitarian, author and President of the United States.)**

It is March 17, 1976.

Since I returned home from the Army I've spent a lot of time taking pictures. I thought that, perhaps, that might be how I could make my living. A parade seemed like a good place to get some interesting shots. A brief subway ride from my Brooklyn neighborhood brought me along with my brother and a couple of his friends to "Mid-Town" to see the Saint Patrick's Day parade. It was a bright and blustery day on the Island of Manhattan in the City of New York.

I had seen the parade before, and although it has exciting moments, it can be, at times, ultimately monotonous with bagpipers playing the same "auld" songs one after the other for hours on end. Having taken a number of pictures, I sat down on the curb and somberly watched, elbows on knees, palms of hands and fingers on cheeks, as the parade passed me by.

Suddenly, I saw Jimmy Carter. He was marching along with some local Democratic party dignitaries and causing quite a bit of excitement amongst the crowd. I sprang up, camera in hand, and hustled out into the center of the street just a few paces before him. He stopped to give me time to get a good picture. I took two before the guards around him shooed me away.

That was the first time I had a good look at him, and that was true of the vast majority of the people along the parade route, too. In fact, many of them had never heard of Jimmy Carter. He seemed to have come out of nowhere. This fact helped his chances to achieve his goal, the Presidency of the United States.

Following the Watergate scandal, Americans had become eager to have someone who was completely different in the White House, someone who was not tainted by the insider politics of Washington, D.C.

The country had just gone through some very difficult years that included brutal assassinations, The Vietnam War and then on top of everything else, Watergate. In addition, the costs of our industrial society were catching up with America, including pollution and the problems that went along with our growing dependency on foreign oil. People began to wonder if America could ever fully recover.

Jimmy Carter had a common touch that people could trust. He was refreshingly honest and brought with him hope for renewal to a beleaguered nation. He also possessed a gentle and peaceful side that spelled relief to a country still weary of war.

The four years after his election saw wonderful triumphs and devastating defeats. This book recounts those years, but it also looks at his unlikely path to the White House and the contributions made by Carter in the decades following his return to his home in rural Georgia. It also closely examines some of the people in his life that helped to mold his destiny; particularly his beloved family members and friends but also his foes. Carter's is a uniquely American story worth knowing by everyone.

Chapter I

LASTING IMPRESSIONS

"When one tugs at a single thing in nature, he finds it attached to the rest of the world." – John Muir (American naturalist and author.)

It is the height of summer, 1937.

The Georgia sun shone like a dazzling orange ball in a clear blue sky. Far down below is a farm with bright green grass and red dirt. In the farmhouse yard white sand lines the walkway to the wooden steps leading to the back door and the screened-in porch.

The house has a long narrow hallway with rooms on either side - a kitchen with a huge black iron stove and room for a table for breakfast, a dining room with five chairs around the table, a bathroom with a hanging bucket with holes in the bottom to create a shower and bedrooms for the children and their parents. A wooden box telephone is on the wall with a black mouthpiece speaker, a hand crank and receiver hanging on the side.

In the front of the house, in the living room, he lie stretched out flat on his back, his daily chores completed forty-five minutes earlier. Shirtless and barefoot as usual he is wearing an old pair of blue jeans. His build may best be described as wiry and he is just a tad short for his age, nearly thirteen, with reddish hair cropped close.

1

He raised his right hand slowly and brushed away a tiny black gnat that was buzzing, buzzing, buzzing around his ear. Then he brought his arm to rest again by his side. He tried to keep his movements to an absolute minimum. It was hot, already 92 degrees.

If he remained perfectly still he would be cool lying there on the wooden floor of the living room a few feet from the cold brick fireplace. The front door was open to the screened-in porch and straight down the hall the door to the back porch was also open. Every now and then he would luxuriate in a slight and gentle breeze that drifted through the house.

He held a book a foot from his eyes. He couldn't remember when he first became an avid reader but he could easily recall his mother having encouraged him to read and then read some more. Even at the table she would frown with disapproval if he didn't have some reading material in front of him while he ate his meal.

This morning was different. His father was out taking care of business. His mother, a registered nurse, was caring for a neighbor's sick child. His younger sisters Ruth and Gloria were spending time with their friends from school in Plains, the town about three miles to the east, and his infant brother was at their aunt's. The fact that he was all alone, however, was not what made this morning particularly uncommon.

Daddy, a very frugal man, had given him special permission to listen to the family's radio. There was no electricity on the farm and the radio had to be run by battery. To conserve energy it was played but sparingly. This morning his favorite band was performing in a rare daytime broadcast. Relaxed, he closed his eyes for a few seconds to relish the final strains of the band's last melody.

When the show concluded he laid down his book, slowly rose and walked forward three short steps, reached for the knob and switched the radio to the "off" position. He stood erect for a moment then turned his head and looked out of the window, across the porch and into the front yard. He was still savoring the pleasure of the music which had completely relaxed him and nearly transported him into a trance-like state. At that moment a diesel locomotive train clamored and roared by just beyond the front yard pulling a passenger car and a freight car. He did not flinch as would surprised guests. In fact, he was almost completely unaware of the train because he had gotten so used to its frequent runs past the house.

"You comin?" Instantly he stopped thinking about his beloved music. "Hey, you comin o not? Fish ain't gonna come ta you, you know." He turned toward the hall. He recognized the voice of his friend, A.D. Davis, who had just walked over from his house across the road.

A.D. stood in the backyard with a broad smile on his face and a horde of gnats swarming around his head like a black halo. He was black, bigger than average, barefoot, wearing an old grey button-down shirt and black trousers. He was holding a fishing pole in his left hand and in the other he held a small bucket of bait consisting of crickets, worms and caterpillars. "You bet, Ah'm comin."

He turned and forgetting the heat dashed down the hall to his room. Glancing to the right he glimpsed, on the bed, a letter from his Uncle Tom that he received two days before. He had read it over and over again. Tom was a Navy man who sailed to unusual places like Hawaii and China, light years, it seemed, from this little farming community of Archery. Whenever he read one of Uncle Tom's letters he imagined how wonderful it would be to be able to see the world. Some nights he would fall asleep envisioning those distant places about which his Uncle wrote so vividly. How grand it would be to observe first hand the seemingly endless open seas, black beached volcanic islands, flying fish and beautiful exotic people.

Then he looked to the left and there leaning against the wall in the corner of his bedroom was his fishing pole. He grabbed it, headed out the door, then turned and was about to step onto the back porch. Suddenly he stopped dead in his tracks and stood for a second as if thunderstruck. He spun around and ran up the hallway, coming to a halt a few feet before the front door at a wooden table he and his sisters ironically referred to as "Mother".

Known throughout the community as Miz Lillian, their mother was so frequently away at work that sometimes the children did not see much of her for days on end. Often she would come home for just a few hours to bathe and change her clothes and then rush back out again, leaving a list of chores on this table. Luckily, today there was no list because she hadn't been home long enough to write one. Freedom!

He all but flew back down the hall, across the porch and out the door to his waiting buddy who bellowed, "Le's go!" A large bright yellow and black butterfly hovered above them as the friends marched off, the hot sandy ground beneath their feet, towards a creek on the other end of the 360 acre farm. Jimmy felt the heat from the blazing sun on his light-colored skin as the gnats now swarmed around his head too.

They strode alongside a field where various vegetables were being grown for the family and for some of the farm workers. Just a few yards away Jack Clark moved very slowly among the sweet potatoes pulling down on the brim of his straw hat to shade his black face. With a hand on his chin he judiciously reflected upon the state of the crop. The boys shouted a greeting to this powerfully built man, the supervisor of the farm, whom they admired above almost everyone else. It seemed to them that he knew it all when it came to horses, cows, mules and the myriad duties that he faithfully carried out every single day of the week, every week of the year. Jack slowly raised his head and acknowledged the boys with a slight nod and a quick grin, then returned to his task.

Yes, Jack was great. No doubt about that, but Jimmy's highest admiration was reserved for Jack's wife, Rachel. She was *the* one. Small and quiet with light brown skin, almost everyone who knew her said she was "the sweetest, kindest, most caring person" that they had ever met. She could take a quick look at someone and say, "Honey, is dere sumptin wron wit cha taday?" She could read distress in a person's face and when the problem was explained to her she might say in a slow and quiet tone, "Honey, the Lor will take caya a it. You don know when o' how and cha migh haf ta put up wit it fer a bait but da Lor will take caya a it." Right after speaking with her they'd kind of forget what their worry was.

On long treks through the woods, on the way to some secret fishing hole, she would carefully point out the different animals and explain the important singularities of their behavior, such as the curling up and playing dead trick that opossums use to dupe their predators and the workings of the quill defense mechanism of the porcupine. In addition, she might say something like, "You see tha flowah ovah dere? You see it righ ovah dere, the white one, wit the five petals an the yeller in the middle? Tha dere's the Cherakee rose. Its Georgia's own flowah, the Cherakee rose is." After walking a while longer in silence she might say, "Tha tree is call the magnolia." She'd explain that all of the beauty and gifts that nature offers bring with them the responsibility of caring for the earth. Our concern and our care is the price we must pay for nature's countless offerings.

It was the wise and loving Rachel who infused in the youngster a life-long reverence for nature that would be carried all the way to the highest seat of power. She was attentive and generous with her time to a boy whose own mother was often too busy caring for other people's children to provide the attention for which his active mind and decent heart hungered.

Now the ground was crimson clay and he stared down at it as the two boys walked along. Searching... searching ...searching... then, "Yes!" A small pointed piece of flint was poking up from the soil. He bent over quickly and snatched the arrowhead from its resting place. Immediately he seemed to be transported back hundreds of years to a time when the Creek Indians roamed this same land hunting for prey.

He imagined an Indian, perhaps a young boy like himself, shooting an arrow at a large, antlered, running deer and then losing sight of the projectile as it missed its mark and sailed harmlessly into the woods, piercing the earth's surface. Slowly, as the years passed, the shaft of the arrow decayed and ultimately completely disintegrated. European settlers came with their slaves and cleared the woods and began to farm the land. The arrowhead remained buried until a heavy rainfall the night before had gently washed the soil away and it was at last revealed. "Man, you always fine dose. Nobody fines dem bettah. Yeah, nobody." said A.D. with awe. The response was a brief laugh and then a beaming smile as he slipped the arrowhead into his pocket.

They walked into a small patch of woods. A rustling of brush caught their attention. On the ground a few feet in front and to the right was a fairly large reddish-brown bird with a yellow iris and a black pupil, a long tail and striped breast. Clenched in his thin black beak was a small, struggling lizard. The bird, a brown thrasher, noticed the boys and quickly disappeared into the brush with his prize squirming helplessly in his somewhat curved beak.

7

Then the boys followed a path that led a few more yards down to the creek. They sat side by side on a log beneath a tall live oak tree, perhaps 75' high, its branches peacefully overhanging the water. The two baited their hooks with caterpillars and dropped the lines into the swiftly moving current. They were sure they'd catch plenty of catfish and bass. Just then, a snapping turtle slowly appeared from beneath the log that the boys were sitting on and crept silently forward until splashing into the creek. Here it was cool and quiet and peaceful and beautiful. The lazy afternoon slowly elapsed and their catch mounted.

Then he thought he heard a far away voice. At first he couldn't understand what was being said. Turning his head and looking over his left shoulder he listened hard. After a few seconds he recognized the voice as that of Jack Clark and realized that he was calling to him, "Jim-a, Jim-a yer daddy wants you. C'mon dere's sumptin important you haf ta do, Jim-a Cartah."

Chapter II

STRIVING FOR APPROVAL

"We shouldn't ever kill anything that we don't need for food." - James Earl Carter, Sr. (Farmer, businessman, politician and family man.)

It is Fall, 1937.

Jimmy walked out the front door of his house and down the three steps. He carried his lunch, ham on a biscuit and a sweet potato, in a brown paper bag in one hand. In the other hand he grasped a few school books. He followed the dirt path the 50 feet or so to the main road. His two sisters had run up the path after him yet he was oblivious to their presence. The three stood, for about one minute, side by side and waited silently on this cool and overcast early morning.

Then with a roar and a great cloud of dust the rickety yellow school bus pulled up in front of the trio. Jimmy boarded and sat alone by a window. He had now entered into a completely different world from the farm in Archery. Most notably, there are no black people here. Further, in this world he is a shy and quiet boy. Through the dust-covered window he spied A.D. in the distance, sleepy eyed, walking to the "colored" school. Jimmy instinctively waved but his friend could not see him.

The "cracker box", as the bus was derisively known, rumbled forward past an open field and in the distance Jimmy could make out the silhouette of his father standing beneath a slate grey sky and giving instructions to Jack Clark. A small circle of field hands stood by a few yards away talking quietly among themselves, every so often looking up at the clouds, one smoking a cigarette. They were, apparently, waiting for orders. His father was the boss.

Daddy, as Jimmy called him, was about 5'8", 175 pounds, in his mid-forties, stocky and extremely strong, with an eternally sunburned face and reddish hair. Known as Mister Earl by most folks James Earl Carter, Sr. was tough both as a boss and as a father. He simply would not stand for laziness, tardiness, disobedience or dishonesty. Daddy was also the one in charge in the house and when it came to Jimmy he demanded nothing less than perfection.

Once, as a small child, Jimmy stole a penny from the collection plate at church. When Daddy learned of this he took a long flexible peach tree switch and beat the boy's legs. Jimmy experienced a half dozen such whippings during his childhood, whippings that would leave an indelible mark on his psyche. When he was particularly angry with his son he'd call him Jimmy instead of his friendly nickname for him, Hot, short for hot shot.

There was no question but that Mister Earl was a stern disciplinarian. However, Jimmy always thought him to be fair and just. Daddy looked for balance in all things. He felt that every person, every animal, everything had a purpose and should be utilized to its fullest. He taught Jimmy thrift and that waste was a failing.

On the farm, Jimmy worked extremely hard, often alongside the even harder-working Mister Earl. The youngster wanted nothing more than to be useful and to impress his Daddy and win his approval. Jimmy tried with everything he had to live up to his Daddy's expectations. After all, he idolized the man.

The bus barreled on and in the dust and distance his father and the farm became smaller and gradually drifted away and out of sight. He thought of the night before when he sat on the floor in the living room with the radio playing classical music and the volume set to "low", though he was not listening.

Daddy sat, aloof, in his chair near the fireplace, reading the newspaper by the light of the kerosene lamp on the stand beside him. He had gazed at his father. After a while Daddy set the paper down and picked up a copy of Edgar Rice Burroughs' novel *Tarzan's Quest*. He opened the book and without saying a word or even looking up began to read. Jimmy wanted to tell him how much he loved him but he knew that it wasn't the time. Daddy must not be disturbed now.

It was when they went hunting or fishing together that Jimmy felt closest to him. Mister Earl was a great outdoorsman and very much wanted for Jimmy to share in his enthusiasm. He thought that there was great value in hunting and fishing. Mister Earl grew up in a rural environment where hunting was nearly a necessity. He taught Jimmy that he should never kill anything that he didn't need for food.

Jimmy took immense pride in being able to bring supper home for the family. His father would beam with pleasure at his boy's success. They'd ride together in a pick up truck to the hunt and Jimmy would feel a real sense of connection. He never felt his father's love more than when they were in the field, on the hunt.

When hunting doves Jimmy's main job was to spot where Daddy's birds fell and then to run and pick them up when other birds were not coming in. Daddy always set a limit on the number of birds he wanted and having achieved his goal would end the hunt. As he grew older Jimmy thought about how his father's training had also made him adept at shooting.

The bus hit a bump and Jimmy was abruptly brought back to the present. They rumbled past the old cemetery on the left and then he overheard two boys talking. "Ah saw hur in the winder. She was wearin a white dress an holdin a candle like she was lookin fer sumptin." Jimmy knew right away that they were talking about the haunted house on the right. It was presently the home of a local doctor but was far more famous for its ghosts. The boy continued, "You know about the black dawg don cha?" "No", his friend responded excitedly. "Well, he'd appeah every now an den but if you tried ta pet em yer hand would pass right through em." "Wow wee."

The bus continued its short journey into Plains and finally on to the high school grounds. It rolled to a stop and everyone clamored off. Jimmy's sister Ruth instantly darted over to her friend Rosalynn Smith to talk. Jimmy glanced quickly at the two and then he dashed briskly up the eight steps to the front door of the large red brick school building with the massive white columns in front. He was greeted by a few of his classmates and they walked together through the front door, down the hall, and then left and into the auditorium.

They took their seats in the center of the hall, the stage directly before them. Miz Julia Coleman sat at a piano on the stage. Mr. Sheffield, the principal, stepped forward and read from the *Bible*, Leviticus 25:23-24. "...the lan is mine, an you are but aliens who haf become my tenants. Therefore, in every part of the country that cha occupy, you must permit the lan ta be redeemed."

As the assembly continued Jimmy could hear muttering from a boy seated behind him.

"If you can talk wit crowds an keep yer virtue, or walk wit kings – nor lose the common touch; If neithah foes nor lovin friens can hurt cha; If all men count wit cha, but none too much;" Jimmy slowly turned and quietly asked, "What are you doin?" "Miz Julia said Ah have ta memorize dis poem by taday and Ah'm practicin. Ah gotta practice." The boy, with his big eyes bulging, continued his recitation under his breath. Jimmy understood perfectly now. When Miz Julia Coleman gave an assignment you made a point of getting it done and it had better be done right. "Yours is the eart an everythin in it, and – which is mo - you'll be a Man my son!"

Jimmy's attention was drawn to the stage where Mr. Simpson was announcing that there would be a meeting of the Future Farmers of America after school in the gym. Then all of the students rose, faced the flag and recited the Pledge of Allegiance. With the conclusion of the pledge everyone hurriedly filed out and rushed off to class.

Jimmy coolly walked into the classroom and quietly took his seat in the second row. He buried his head in his notebook and focused on his lesson. In between classes he saw Mary Jean amble by and he wondered if she would go out with him. He had just recently discovered the pleasures of dating and now he couldn't get enough of girls. He liked the sweet girls of Archery and the alluring girls of Plains. Girls, girls, girls.

When at long last the end of the school day arrived it was with delight that he strode into the gym. On the wall was a poster that read: LEARNING TO DO, DOINGTO LEARN, EARNING TO LIVE, LIVING TO SERVE a motto of the FFA, which teaches that farmers who use their talents and intelligence can reach success. Future farmers are famous for their speech making, learning to work on a team and cooperation.

An hour and a half later as he left the gym, the last school bus long since gone, he began to walk home when he heard a familiar voice speaking gently but firmly. There, listening to Miz Julia, was the boy with the bulging eyes that he had seen earlier. She was telling him how impressed she was with his recital of the poem in class. As Jimmy walked away he could hear her saying what he had heard her say in different ways countless times before; "Remembah, anyone can grow up ta be President of the United States."

CHAPTER III

FILLING THE LARGEST OF SHOES

"Let us follow our destiny, ebb and flow. Whatever may happen, we master fortune by accepting it." - Virgil (Classical Roman poet.)

It is the summer of 1953.

Jimmy had left home when he was barely out of his teens and only returned from time to time for brief stays. He is back once again, standing in the house where he was raised. Now, he is grown up to 5 feet 9 and a half inches and is physically fit. Under almost any other circumstance he would be happy to be here, but today is completely different. Daddy has died. Jimmy has returned to pay his respects and help with the arrangements for the funeral service and burial.

Standing alone in the living room that is so familiar to him, he begins to think about when he was, eagerly, entering the United States Naval Academy at Annapolis, Maryland. He so desperately wanted to go to sea so that he could have many wonderful and amazing adventures like Uncle Tom Gordy. Jimmy's high level of motivation paid off and, after first studying at Georgia Southwestern in nearby Americus, he met with great success in the Academy.

He decided that, right after graduation, he would get married. As a teenager he had gone out on more than his fair share of dates. He craved girls, with all of his heart. His interest stemmed from his earliest days in Archery when he would watch the mocha skinned pretty young girls with their tightly coiled hair and lackadaisical ways, giggling and strolling barefoot in the dusty sunshine through Daddy's fields. He went out with most of the girls in his High School at one time or another, and by the time he was in college he was dating the most beautiful of the coeds, including Miss Georgia Southwestern. In Jimmy's mind, however, none could compare with Rosalynn Smith.

Only about three miles from where Jimmy stood was the home of the Smiths, in Plains. The family had very little money, but that didn't much matter because they were, for the most part, self sufficient. They grew much of their own food and kept a few animals for milk, eggs, and for slaughter. Her mother made Rosalynn's clothes for her of which she was pleased and proud.

She was a deeply religious Christian who did not drink alcohol and never even considered smoking cigarettes (in part because her father told her that women who smoked were "ugly").

Rosalynn was an introverted girl who would sometimes look at her face in the mirror, fingertips touching her cheek, head tilted slightly to one side and, almost involuntarily, whisper one word, "Ordinary."

When she was small there happened to be no girls in Plains and although she played with boys, she found that she was often quite lonesome. She took solace in reading books about far away places and, like Jimmy, dreamed of some day seeing them for herself. On the advice of her 7th grade teacher she read the newspaper and listened to the radio in an effort to broaden her horizons. She was a straight "A" student who loved math and science.

When, in high school, she finally met some girls she could befriend, she happened to choose Ruth Carter, Jimmy's sister. She was spending the night with Ruth in Archery when Miz Lillian woke her from a deep sleep to tell her that her father had died and to take her home. Miz Lillian had been helping out by going every day to Rosalynn's father to administer shots and assist her mother in caring for him as he, suffering from leukemia, slowly, painfully, wasted away. He was only forty-four years old when he died, and Rosalynn was but thirteen.

She had to help her mother raise her two younger brothers and a sister. Despite everything, she managed to graduate from Plains High School as valedictorian and went on to attend Georgia Southwestern.

Suddenly, one day, she noticed a picture hanging on the wall in Ruth's room. It was a picture that she had seen dozens of times before but, at the same time, never *really* saw. It was a photograph of Jimmy. She instantly fell in love with it, and with him...forever.

When Jimmy was home on leave she went with him and Ruth to the Pond House for a picnic and to clean up. The Pond House was a few miles from town and was built by Mr. Earl to be used for parties and picnics. She found that she was not at all shy with Jimmy as she was with other boys. Together, they swept the house, raked the yard and talked. He was 20 and she 17.

That night he pulled up in front of the church and asked her to go out on a double date with him, Ruth and her boyfriend, and she answered, "Yes." The next morning Jimmy told Miz Lillian that he was going to marry Rosalynn Smith. A few months later he proposed, and she again answered, "Yes."

After the Naval Academy they married, and Jimmy was assigned to an oil-leaking old battleship named the USS Wyoming in Norfolk, Virginia. As one of the lowest ranking officers, he was among the last to receive time off. When he could get home he had an intense love affair with Rosalynn. Soon they had their first son, Jack.

After a while he asked to be and was assigned to the dangerous submarine division of the Navy. Before he knew it, he found himself deep beneath the surface of the ocean on a constant Cold War patrol for Soviet ships. Then he was transferred to the paradise of Pearl Harbor, Hawaii. Rosalynn learned to hula and would dance while Jimmy played the ukelele. James Earl Carter III was soon born, and they called him Chip.

Jimmy was at sea for months at a time in a submarine that was a claustrophobic steel tube with the recycled air often smelling of cigarettes, diesel fuel, body odor and vomit. Carter would listen for hours to the seemingly endless sounds on the sonar device for signs of enemy ships and, incidentally, was treated to the the high pitched squeal of dolphins and the peaceful, mesmerizing and otherworldly songs of gigantic humpback whales.

The USS Pomfret was an early submarine assignment, an older boat that had served in World War II. Two days after Christmas in 1948 he departed on a long cruise to the western reaches of the

Pacific Ocean. Several ships were lost in very difficult weather. He was seasick for five straight days.

One night, while the sub was skimming on the surface of the pitch black ocean, Jimmy stood watch. Water splashed in his face as waves crashed violently over the deck of the sub. Standing alone, his hands gripped with all of his might the iron pipe handrail as a fierce storm raged around him. Then, suddenly, a giant wave raced across the deck of the ship, engulfing Jimmy and forcing his hands from the railing. The water raised him up and for a few seconds he was swirling hopelessly inside the wave. Then, as suddenly as it appeared, the wave receded and deposited him on top of a gun on the rear of the sub. He grasped the barrel for dear life and after a few seconds gingerly lowered himself to the deck and he staggered back to his station having, just barely, cheated death.

Then came what he thought to be the chance of his lifetime. An unusual man was starting an amazing new project, and Jimmy wanted very much to be a part of it. The man, Hyman Rickover, was a visionary. He was also a tough and unsmiling perfectionist with zero tolerance for ignorance.

A wiry figure with his white hair parted almost down the middle, this Captain, and later four-star Admiral, had a dream of a navy whose ships were powered by the recently harnessed nuclear energy. All told he would serve in the Navy for 63 years, the longest serving naval officer in U.S. History. He would become known as the "Father of the Nuclear Navy."

He was born in 1900 into a Jewish family in Poland who migrated together to the United States in 1905 in order to escape persecution by anti-semites. They first lived on the East Side of Manhattan, but after 2 years they moved to Chicago. He started working at nine years old holding a light as his neighbor operated a machine. He earned 3 cents an hour.

After High School he attended The United States Naval Academy in Annapolis. He further earned a Master's Degree in electrical engineering. He sought duty on submarines and eventually became commander on two.

In 1941, after the Japanese bombed Pearl Harbor and hurled the U.S. headlong into World War II, Rickover was ordered there to organize repairs of the electrical power plant of the U.S.S. California. He soon gained a reputation as a no non-sense leader who knew how to get things done.

His remarkable intellect and dedication moved him quickly into the program that developed the world's first use of atomic power for the production of electricity, and the propulsion of ships. In 1946 Rickover volunteered to go to what is now the Oak Ridge National Laboratory to help develop a nuclear electric generating plant. He became the deputy manager of the entire project. He soon became a devotee of nuclear marine propulsion.

In 1949 he assumed control of the Navy's effort as Director of the Naval Reactors Branch in the Bureau of Ships. He lead the effort to develop the world's first nuclear-powered submarine, the USS

Nautilus, which was launched and commissioned in 1954. Jimmy applied to be one of the first to serve in this revolutionary new navy.

Rickover ordered him into his office and subjected him to an intense interview lasting over two hours. Finally, Rickover asked about Jimmy's career in the Naval Academy, and he (ever honest) had to admit that although he finished high up in his class, he did not always do his best. Rickover's face was stern, cold and deadly serious as he looked straight into Jimmy's eyes. Then he chillingly turned his back to him and tersely asked, "Why not?" Rickover then resumed some paper work he had been toiling over when Jimmy had first walked in.

He could find no answer and then he slowly and quietly exited the office. Jimmy was at a loss. "Why *not* the best?" he had to ask himself dejectedly as the door creaked and swung closed behind him and with it, he believed, his chances.

However, Rickover, to Jimmy's astonishment, did accept him into the program and he was transferred to Schenectady, New York, where he would study nuclear physics in the graduate program at Union College, becoming a nuclear engineer. He was then assigned the duty of directing the construction of one of the nation's first nuclear submarines, The U.S.S. Sea Wolf. Jimmy worked closely with, but under, Rickover whom he both feared and respected like no one else except his own father. Rickover personally oversaw every detail of his command, a trait that Carter would embrace for the rest of his own career.

One day Rickover said to Jimmy's surprise, "I wish that nuclear power had never been discovered." Jimmy blurted out, "Admiral, this is your life." The old salt said, "I would forego all the accomplishments of my life, and I would be willing to forgo all the advantages of nuclear power to propel ships, for medical research and for every other purpose of generating electric power, if we could have avoided the evolution of atomic explosives."

Jimmy's keen knowledge of nuclear power resulted in an invitation to help to solve an extremely dangerous situation. A nuclear reactor had melted down in a Canadian research facility, and some radioactive material was released into the atmosphere. Jimmy was asked to go to Chalk River in the Ontario Province in Canada to help disassemble the damaged nuclear reactor core. The radiation intensity meant that he could only spend ninety seconds at the hot core location.

An exact duplicate mock up of the reactor was constructed on a nearby tennis court and television cameras monitored the actual damaged equipment far beneath the ground. He and two colleagues practiced on the mock up version and then, wearing protective clothes, they went into the reactor and worked frantically for the allotted time until the reactor was disassembled and rendered harmless.

His naval career was going incredibly well. He was, after-all, in the most exciting part of the service with the greatest promise for advancement. It seemed that his formidable dreams of nautical success were soon to be realized.

Then, suddenly and unexpectedly, he was called home to Archery. Daddy was sick and didn't have much longer to live. He had developed pancreatic cancer. All alone, Jimmy returned to his boyhood home and sat in a large chair in his parent's room alongside his dying father. The two men talked animatedly for hours on end about days gone by together on the farm and of Jimmy's life in the Navy. Jimmy watched as one person after another stopped in to talk to Mr. Earl, mostly just to say what could be boiled down to two very plain and simple words, "Thank you."

When Mr. Earl died Jimmy was dumbfounded by the outpouring of gratitude that people demonstrated to his late father's memory. Mr. Earl was not only a devoted family man and an honest employer, but a generous friend, a community and political leader and a good and loving neighbor.

After all was said and done and Jimmy had returned to Schenectady, he began to reflect upon the meaning of his own life and where he should spend his seemingly boundless energy, discipline and ambition. He wondered, "If I were to die would even one person come to say the kind of words that so many spoke for Daddy?"

Mr. Earl was only 54 years old when he died, and had just been elected to the State Legislature. It seemed to Jimmy that his father had left so much undone and that there were so many promises yet unfulfilled. Then, he thought, "I can do it." He believed that he could achieve the things that his father would have, had he lived. He thought he would take over where Daddy had left off. He would give up the Navy and return home in an effort to begin to earn the love of the people of his community the way his Daddy had. At last Jimmy could become the man he really always wanted to be. He would fill Daddy's shoes.

Chapter IV

FIRST STEPS ON THE ROAD TO HISTORY

"We shall require a substantially new manner of thinking if mankind is to survive." - Albert Einstein (Theoretical physicist.)

To simply say that Rosalynn did not want to go would be the understatement of the century. She loved their life in the Navy. Jimmy, however, was stubbornly adamant and nothing or no one, not even the sobbing, shouting, screaming and scolding Rosalynn could change his mind. He resigned from the Navy, packed his belongings and his family into his car and, with only a small savings, drove South to his home and to his destiny.

When the group arrived in Plains it was with a uniformly sour disposition...with one exception. Jimmy had a huge smile on his face, his large teeth glistening in the blazing Georgia sunlight.

The family's first home was a small apartment in a public-housing project with a rent of just $30. a month. They had three sons now: Jack, Chip and Jeff. Having been away from the farm for so long Jimmy had to learn about developments in agriculture as quickly as possible if he hoped to have any chance of staying in business. He read, watched other farmers, and took courses on farming.

The beginning was rough. A drought their first year back ruined the peanut crop and the family's total income did not quite reach

$200. As they continued to struggle Rosalynn joined in the effort, going to the warehouse and keeping the books of the Carter family business. The following year their fortunes changed. The drought was but a distant memory and business prospered.

With the improvement in income the family moved to a big, old (1850), drafty house on a rural road about a mile from the warehouse. This was the very same house that was believed to be haunted. It was said that Union soldiers who were killed nearby during the Civil War continued to reside in the old structure. As a child Rosalynn would go a considerable distance out of the way in order to avoid walking by the house where she had witnessed flashing lights in the attic when no one was at home.

While they were living there Rosalynn heard something in the attic every night that sent shivers up her spine. Once, when the boys were playing in the attic, they removed some bricks from the floor of the fireplace and discovered a small room. Rosalynn thought that maybe some of the Union soldiers hid in this room and perhaps that's why its believed that they haunt it.

Haunted house aside, it wasn't long before Jimmy was making a name for himself in the community. He became the project chairman of the Lion's Club, the only civic club in town, and that year the town was renewed. He and Rosalynn helped raise money for a community swimming pool that Jimmy designed. Jimmy was soon the director of the county Chamber of Commerce and a member of the Library Board, the Hospital Authority, and the County School Board. He also became a scoutmaster and a deacon in the church. Rosalynn joined the Baptist Church and taught Sunday school as did Jimmy.

Jimmy broke Plains tradition and closed the warehouse on Saturday afternoons so they could go camping and spend more time with their quickly growing boys. They enjoyed adventures and many outdoor activities as a family. Each year they went fishing in Florida with their friends and all of their children. Once he and Rosalynn flew to Cuba with reservations for one night and stayed for two, leaving at 5 a.m. the second morning after staying up all night.

But harsh reality was never really far away, especially when the Supreme Court had ruled in 1954 in the case of Brown v. Board of Education that public schools should be integrated. The decision caused Jimmy serious angst: "Ah don't know what's goin to happen aroun here."

In the navy Jimmy had lived and worked on an equal basis with black sailors. His father had believed, sincerely, that segregation was best for everyone. Miz Lillian, on the other hand, had nursed whomever needed her, black or white, and Jimmy tended to identify with her ideology.

In 1894 the Supreme Court decided the case of Plessy v. Ferguson, in which a man who was partially black was denied the right to sit in a white section of a train because there was an "equal" black section for him to use. The Southern States, including Georgia, developed a series of laws that intended to keep black people and white people separated in order to create an environment of white supremacy.

These laws were called Jim Crow after a 19th Century cartoon/ minstrel character of a stereotypical black man.

Under the Jim Crow laws interracial marriage was strictly forbidden, black people could not vote, they could not use the same public facilities as white people, and they were discriminated against in their efforts to attain decent employment. Though the public facilities were separate, they were almost never equal. For example, the State of Georgia spent four times as much on an individual white student as it did on a black student.

If a black man was thought to have violated any of the laws, he might have been subjected to a lynching. That is to say, hung. The fact is that hundreds of black people were lynched in Georgia during the Jim Crow era. White people who violated the code faced arrest, ostracism and the hate of their neighbors and so called friends. It was in this atmosphere that several forces interacted to change the course of American history.

The White Citizens Council was formed in the 1950's to oppose racial integration. They resisted court ordered integration through boycotts, denial of loans, and other pressure methods. They claimed to be different from the Ku Klux Klan because they used non-violent means to their desired end. However, violence sometimes ensued if their other methods failed.

Medgar Evers was a World War II veteran and attended college on the GI bill. He was a black civil rights activist working for the National Association for the Advancement of Colored People

(NAACP) in Mississippi. Evers had traveled across Mississippi getting black people to register to vote and recruiting them into the Civil Rights movement.

He was instrumental in getting witnesses and evidence for the murder case of Emmett Till, a 14 year old black boy who had been murdered for talking to a white woman, which brought national attention to the plight of African Americans in the South. Evers had interviewed citizens who were intimidated by the council to prepare affidavits for use as evidence against the council. He was an extremely strong worker in the Civil Rights movement. He set up boycotts against whites whose businesses discriminated. In addition, he helped James Meredith to be the first black person to gain entry to the University of Mississippi.

After John F. Kennedy's administration provided support for Meredith to register at the University, Kennedy appeared on national television to speak to the issue of racial inequality saying:

It ought to be possible, therefore, for American students of any color to attend any public institution they select without having to be back-ed up by troops. It ought to to be possible for American consumers of any color to receive equal service in places of public accommodation, such as hotels and restaurants and theaters and retail stores, without being forced to resort to demonstrations in the street, and it ought to be possible for American citizens of any color to register and to vote in a free election without interference or fear of reprisal. It ought to be possible, in short, for every American to enjoy the privileges of being American without regard to his race or his color. In short, every American ought to have the right to be treated as he would wish to be treated, as one would wish his children to be treated. But this is not the case. We are confronted primarily with a moral issue. It is as old as the Scriptures and is as clear as the American Constitution.

The heart of the question is whether all Americans are to be afforded equal rights and equal opportunities, whether we are going to treat our fellow Americans as we want to be treated. If an American, because his skin is dark, cannot eat lunch in a restaurant open to the public, if he cannot send his children to the best public school available, if he cannot vote for the public officials who will represent him, if, in short, he cannot enjoy the full and free life which all of us want, then who among us would be content to have the color of his skin changed and stand in his place? Who among us would then be content with the counsels of patience and delay?

President Kennedy went on to say that he would introduce legislation to Congress that would enforce the civil rights of all Americans.

Just hours after the President's speech, at 12:50 a.m. on June 12, 1963, a member of the White Citizens Council, Byron De La Beckwith, hid in a clump of honeysuckle vines across from Medgar Evers' house. De La Beckwith was clutching a high powered .30-06 Enfield hunting rifle.

Medgar Evers was carrying NAACP T-shirts that read "Jim Crow Must Go" when he stepped out of his car and into the driveway that led to his small wood and brick one story home. De La Beckwith aimed with care, squeezed the trigger and discharged one shot. The bullet passed through Evers' body leaving a large wound in his back. The shot continued onward and through the front window of his house where his wife and three small children were anxiously awaiting his return home. Evers managed to crawl to his front doorstep where his wife discovered his bleeding body moments later. In less than an hour Medgar was pronounced dead at a nearby hospital.

A short six months later President Kennedy, himself, would die after being gunned down by a sniper. However, the outrage over Evers' death helped to spark support for legislation that would become the Civil Rights Act of 1964.

It was in this atmosphere that the City of Atlanta was racked with sit-ins, demonstrations, and boycotts as other barriers - segregation in waiting rooms and restrooms, at lunch counters and drinking fountains - were challenged. The issue was moving closer and closer to rural Georgia, where the general attitude was still, "No, not one!" Meaning no integration whatsoever.

When Jimmy served on the Board of Education he learned that most of the old inequalities remained. The black children had no buses and still had to walk to school. Their textbooks and typewriters were old discards from the white schools, and the quality of education overall for the blacks was far inferior. He began to publicly express his concerns.

Jimmy was working quietly one day at the warehouse when the local chief of police and the depot agent, who was also a Baptist preacher, walked in and invited him to join the White Citizens Council. He refused to join, but they persisted, even offering to pay the $5. dues for him if that was what was holding him back. They claimed that he was the only adult white male in the community that did not join, yet, he still refused. Then they threatened to organize a boycott of his business.

At church on Sundays some of the Carter's 'friends' shunned them. One night on their way home from a basketball game they noticed a simple sign on the warehouse door that read "COONS AND CARTER GO TOGETHER."

One day, soon afterward, about twenty of his best customers showed up and encouraged Jimmy to join the Council or else face the loss of business. Again they offered to pay the $5. annual dues. Jimmy cooly walked to the cash register, opened it and pulled out a $5. bill. "Ah'll take this and flush it down the toilet, but Ah am not gonna join the White Citizen's Council."

But the boycott failed to materialize, with one or two minor exceptions - one being Rosalynn's cousin, who never came back to the office again. Jimmy's later commitment to human rights came, in part, from his personal knowledge of the devastating effect of racial segregation in his region of the country.

On the morning of his thirty-eighth birthday he got up, put on his Sunday best, and casually told Rosalynn that he was going to register to run for a seat in the Georgia Senate. Then on primary day Jimmy went from one polling place to another and quickly discovered why elections in nearby Quitman County always went the way of the county political boss, Sheriff Joe Hurst. There were no voting booths, and everyone was marking ballots in public while Mr. Hurst or one of his goons looked on with an intimidating stare. Jimmy's protests were completely ignored, and he called a friend to come and watch the polls for him. That didn't help either.

On election, night, when returns came in from every County except Quitman, he was leading by 70 votes. The political bosses in Quitman County decided to change the results, and when their returns finally came in, although in one case 330 people had actually voted, there were 430 votes counted. The Hurst group recorded votes of deceased people and used other dirty tricks. It appeared that Jimmy had lost the election.

But he would not take "no" for an answer and demanded an investigation and a recount, even in the face of threats to his safety and the safety of his family and warehouse. Finally a judge confirmed the fraud and Jimmy was duly elected to the Senate. He had just begun a political journey down a road that that would ultimately lead to the Oval Office.

CHAPTER V

THE PRODIGAL SON

"He said to him, 'My son, you are here with me always; everything I have is yours. But now we must celebrate and rejoice, because your brother was dead and has come to life again; he was lost and has been found.'" - Luke 15:31-32

One day, soon after Jimmy's return to his hometown, while he was visiting his mother, he and Miz Lillian stood together talking quietly just inside the closed back screen door of her house. They could see a tough looking, muscular, sixteen year old boy with a long face and a thick head of hair, just twenty yards away, slowly, dejectedly, pacing back and forth with his hands stuffed down deeply into his pockets, his head hung low and his shoulders slumped forward.

Jimmy stopped talking, paused, then hung his own head. Miz Lillian could not tell if the look on his face was one of pity, remorse, shame or regret, but she said, "Now Jim-a, don you dare fret, don you dare. It isn't yer fault. He'll be okay in time. You'll see. You haf ta foller yer heart. You always haf ta foller yer heart. It's yer duty, Jim-a. Yer duty. You understan?" "Yes, of course Ah do, mama. Of course, Ah do." A moment later when they looked up and out the door again the teen had vanished.

The boy walked with great haste toward the peanut fields with which he was so intimately familiar. A gust of wind blew up and red dust covered his rugged and good looking face. He kept walking, lumbering along oblivious to everything around him, until he at last reached the center of the huge field. He sat down in the dirt and was certain that he was far enough away so that no one would see or hear him. Sitting crossed legged, his hands on his knees, he glared up at the deep blue sky. He was completely quiet and perfectly still for a long moment.

Then, unexpectedly, it happened, tears began to pool up in his eyes. One leaked out and slowly trickled down his left check leaving a distinct trail through the dust on his face. Next, they began to flow out uncontrollably until his whole face was a mix of tears and of dirt. He didn't even try to stop the crying. Because his pain was so great he wished he could somehow let it all out. He knew, however, that no matter how hard he cried, or for how long, the pain would not go away. Not ever.

While continuing to look up to the sky he shouted imploringly, "Why? Why'd cha haf ta leave me? Why'd cha haf ta die fer?" He was so lonesome in the vast and empty field. There was no one there to console him. No one to say to him that it would be "alright." Anyhow, no one could have consoled him, his agony was so great. Not even his thirteen year old girlfriend, Sybil.

Not only did he lose the most important man in his life, when Mr. Earl died, but he lost his future when Jimmy came home unexpectedly. "Now, wha? Wha's ta become a me?" Billy Carter wondered out loud through his almost unbearable torment and tears.

Billy physically resembled Mr. Earl and even had many of the same subtle and not so subtle mannerisms. He had been much closer to Daddy than even Jimmy had ever been. His father spoiled Billy, allowing him a long leash and ready forgiveness for his mistakes unlike the more disciplined treatment Jimmy had experienced at his father's tutelage.

Billy worked side by side with his father from the time he was very small until Mr. Earl became too debilitated by cancer to work. Billy always believed that running the farm was to be his future. His father had painstakingly taken him through every last aspect of farming life and the boy never would have guessed, even in ten million years, that Jimmy would come home, uninvited, and snatch the mantle of responsibility from his shoulders. A responsibility that by all rights was positively his.

But Billy knew that he could not beat Jimmy. It would be an impossibility. Jimmy had always been a remote, unreal character to Billy, like a figure from a book that could not be touched or changed. Yes, that's it, it would be like trying to change the behavior of a character in one of the dozens of books that Billy was so fond of reading. It just could not be done.

Meanwhile, Jimmy had not even given much thought to how his actions would effect his fragile younger brother. Jimmy was thirteen years older than Billy and left for the Navy when Billy was just a small boy far too young to do any type of farm work. When home on his leaves, Jimmy would spend very little time with his junior sibling. Most of the hours of his precious few free days were spent with his old friends from school, his closest relatives, or with his parents. And now Jimmy could not even begin to imagine letting his younger brother's wishes come before what he so firmly believed was his destiny.

Now Billy had to work for his big brother, and he absolutely hated it, his rage even manifesting itself in fist fights between the two. He sought to try to silence the demons that haunted his almost every conscious moment. It wasn't long before he found that drinking beer appeared to help to squelch the pain, and that sometimes the more potent moonshine would seem to soothe him when beer wasn't quite doing the trick. Smoking non-filtered cigarettes and getting drunk would serve as his self-prescribed anesthetic.

The one person that he could always count upon for solace, encouragement and support was the one and only love of his life, Sybil. Sybil Spires and her family had come to Plains from Clayton, Alabama in 1948, and when she was ten years old she met Billy at a baseball game. By the time that she was eleven Billy announced that he wanted to marry her. In return for his devotion to her she helped him to, somewhat, curb his fury and encouraged him to have a little faith in the future.

But even with Sybil's patient love, Billy developed into a hell raising trouble maker. And so he became the boy that mothers told their sons to stay away from. Even though he was on the short side at 5 feet 6 inches, he was always on the look out for a good fight, fights which in the end he would seldom, if ever, win. He was constantly exhibiting foolish behavior, like taking off all of his clothes in icy cold weather and running through the center of the town for the amusement of his pals.

And although he was highly intelligent, it wasn't long before it became apparent that school was a total waste of time for Billy. He was suspended on several occasions and finally settled on just biding his time until graduation and the day he could finally leave Plains for good.

So it was that on the very day after graduation he abruptly left for a four year enlistment in the Marine Corps. He was happy to get away, but when he completed boot camp he did return home just long enough to marry sixteen year old Sybil who dropped out of school to become his wife.

While serving in the Marines he learned how to really do some hard drinking, and it was then that his alcoholism began to truly blossom. In addition, his penchant for fighting and generally getting into trouble with authority figures did not end with his entry into the Corps. On one occasion he cursed out an officer and on another "slugged" a lieutenant. After four years he was still just a lowly private, and it was apparent that the military held no future for this tortured and confused young man.

When he was discharged from the service he, along with Sybil and now two baby girls in tow had little choice but to return to Plains and go back to work for Jimmy. Needless to say, he abhorred every last minute of it.

Sometimes he would get drunk and drive off into the darkness, only to be stopped by the police and made to spend a night or two behind bars. Other displays of public drunkenness might also cause him to end up with a brief stay in jail. He tried to stop drinking, but the grip that alcohol had taken on him, by this time, appeared much too great to allow him to break free.

Again, he fled from Plains bringing with him his precious Sybil and the little ones. He tried attending college but after a year realized that it was clearly just not for him. He worked in a paint factory in Macon, Georgia, for a while and was miserable until one day in 1962 when, out of the clear blue sky, the phone rang.

On the other end of the line was none other than Jimmy. He told Billy that he had decided to enter political life and that he needed someone to help run the farm and the Carter Warehouse so he could have time to give as much attention as possible to the pursuit of his political career.

Billy did not hesitate to return to Plains, and this time he wanted to stay for the rest of his life. He had found hope for the first time in years. Yes, Jimmy would still run the business end of things, but Billy would work with the farmers and other employees directly, giving him the opportunity, at least in part and at long last, to fulfill his dream of taking over for his beloved Daddy.

CHAPTER VI

DETERMINATION

"The sad duty of politics is to establish justice in a sinful world." - Reinhold Niebuhr (Theologian.)

"Destiny is not a matter of change, it is a matter of choice: Destiny is not a thing to be waited for, it is a thing to be achieved." - William Jennings Bryan (Lawyer, Congressman, Secretary of State, three-time Presidential candidate.)

Jimmy served with honor in the State Senate. However, he was largely quiet and tried his best not to ruffle any feathers. It seems that he was learning the ways of the political world. He was biding his time and, at least for the moment, was managing to keep his burning ambitions in check. He was elected to a second two year term and served much as he did in the first. When the second term ended the time was right, he thought, to make a bold move.

Jimmy had decided that he was the one who should be Governor of the State of Georgia. Disciplined and hard driven Jimmy plunged into his campaign. He worked night and day and every member of his family pitched in on the campaign trail. He was perceived as a moderate running against a racist candidate, Lester Maddox.

Maddox a man short of stature, bald and wearing glasses owned a family run Atlanta based restaurant business featuring Southern fried chicken. Following the passage of the Civil Rights Act of 1964

Maddox fought to continue running a Jim Crow style segregated restaurant. He embraced peculiar, although not uncommon, beliefs. He thought, for instance, that blacks were intellectual inferiors to whites and that segregation was justified by the teachings in the Bible.

When three young black customers tried to enter his restaurant they were met with vehement resistance. Maddox himself, carrying a pistol, led a small mob of like minded individuals who were carrying ax handles and drove away the black people shouting, "You no good dirty devils! You dirty Communists!"

Under legal pressure to allow integration Maddox was at last compelled to close his business. But his stand against integration popularized him among racist voters that hated the passage of the Civil Rights Act and he ran for political office. His announcement that he would run for Governor was quickly followed by an endorsement from the Ku Klux Klan.

Although he fought hard Jimmy was ultimately defeated and, quite naturally, extremely depressed. He had lost twenty two pounds during the grueling campaign and his efforts took their toll on his health. Jimmy lost faith in himself and in the political system. He also began to seriously question what God had in store for him in this lifetime.

Jimmy's younger sister, Ruth Stapleton, heard about his disillusionment and came home to Plains to talk to him personally. Now a prominent evangelical preacher Ruth convinced Jimmy that he needed to completely devout himself to Jesus Christ.

Along with other born again Christians Jimmy volunteered to go on what were known as "Pioneer Missions". He traveled to Pennsylvania and working with another man the two knocked on doors. The first man explained the basics of their Christian faith then Jimmy would help by offering scripture readings and then answer related questions.

They had been given a list consisting of one hundred names of people who never attended a religious service of any kind. The two zealots set out to visit all one hundred and to get enough of them to agree to worship together as Baptists.

They stayed in a cheap room and visited all sorts of people; rich and poor, young and old. They managed to convert almost fifty of those they visited. Before leaving town the two men helped the new converts to find a storefront to turn into their own house of worship.

Later Jimmy traveled to other towns with the same mission. With each successful conversion Jimmy's confidence was restored. But now, and forever after, he was driven not by personal ambition or patriotism alone but by his sense of duty to his Lord and savior Jesus Christ.

When Jimmy returned to Plains he was more determined than ever to be elected Governor. Once again he began conducting a highly intense campaign. During the four year period following his defeat Jimmy made over 1,800 speeches. Jimmy and Rosalynn shook over a half a million hands of prospective voters. Even their three boys were hard on the trail. Every one was determined that this time, no matter what, Jimmy was going to win. While on the campaign trail Jimmy had some unusual experiences. One such experience occurred on a night when he was in the little town of Leary, Georgia not too far from Plains. He was waiting to give a speech to a group of people who were members of the popular community service organization, the Lions Club. Jimmy stood outside with a handful of others waiting for the meeting to begin when one man said to him, "Look, ovah in the west." Jimmy looked up and in the distance he saw an object as bright as the moon that was giving off a peculiar looking light and was hovering silently in the sky. The UFO began to change colors from white to red and then to blue. After a while the object began to recede until, at last, it vanished. UFO's aside Jimmy campaigned as the common man, as a "typical" southerner, he was able to capture the support of Georgians and win the nomination of the Democratic party. He went on to handily defeat his Republican opponent in the general election.

A reading of Jimmy's inaugural address makes it clear to anyone, once and for all, the direction that Georgia would take regarding race when he wrote;

> At the end of a long campaign, I believe I know our people as well as anyone. Based on this knowledge of Georgians North and South, rural and urban, liberal and conservative, I say to you quite frankly that the time for racial discrimination is over.
> Our people have already made this major and difficult decision, but we cannot underestimate the challenge of hundreds of minor decisions yet to be made. Our inherent human charity and our religious beliefs will be taxed to the limit. No poor, rural, weak,

or black person should ever have to bear the additional burden of being deprived of the opportunity of an education, a job or simple justice. We Georgians are fully capable of making our judgments and managing our own affairs. We who are strong or in positions of leadership must realize that the responsibility for making correct decisions in the future is ours. As Governor, I will never shirk this responsibility.

Later the speech focused on the natural beauty of his State and the threat that it faced because of "avarice, selfishness, procrastination, and neglect." He recognized that growth and progress require changes but that, "Our challenge is to insure that such activities avoid destruction and dereliction of our environment."

As Governor, Jimmy boldly opposed public works projects that needlessly harmed the environment, such as the construction of large dams simply for the sake of creating work.

He also pressed State Legislators to pass laws to help preserve and protect the environment. He was influential in establishing the Georgia Heritage Trust which was designed to inventory and assess more than two thousand sites to protect them from unnecessary destruction.

The confrontation that met with the most controversy in regard to the protection of the natural beauty of Georgia was with the Army Corp of Engineers. They wished to construct a major dam on Georgia's Flint River about fifty miles southeast of Atlanta. The dam promised to bring with it the ability to generate large amounts of electricity, purify the rivers water, provide for recreation areas as well as control floods.

At first Jimmy found the plan to be promising but further investigation soon caused him to change his point of view. He flew over the proposed site and traveled the river by canoe, twice. He ordered the Engineers to provide him with a detailed report on the costs and projected benefits of the dam. His in depth analysis caused Jimmy to quickly realize that the dam was a wasteful project and was not at all capable of producing the types of benefits that it so grandly promised. When the bill came to his desk in the Governor's mansion for the approval to go ahead with the project Jimmy unhesitatingly vetoed it.

Jimmy managed to cut a significant amount of waste from the Georgia government by reducing the number of different State departments from 300 down to a mere 15. He also encouraged the filming of major motion pictures in the State including Deliverance starring Jon Voigt and The Longest Yard with the star Burt Reynolds.

On occasion he and Rosalynn would take short trips to commune with the wondrous offerings of Georgia's nature. They would canoe or raft its rivers, enjoy fishing and observe the myriad wildlife. They saw red fox, wild pig, raccoons, bears, beaver and marsh rabbit among many other creatures.

Georgia's Constitution did not permit consecutive terms for the Governorship and so in 1975 Jimmy was out of office. This suited him fine because he already had other plans. Jimmy had decided that he was going to be the President of the United States. In 1972 he attended the Democratic National Convention and met all of the potential presidential candidates. He left the convention thinking that he was as good as any of them and that if they could try for the White House why then shouldn't he.

One seeming problem was that Jimmy was not at all well known. In 1973 he appeared on a TV game show called "What's My Line?" in which the contestants tried to guess the occupation of the mystery guest. No one could guess what he did. The idea of Jimmy attaining the highest office in the land sounded so unlikely that when he told Miz Lillian that he was going to run for president she asked, "A wha?"

But it was his very anonymity that, ironically, would propel him to victory. The recent Watergate scandal caused many Americans to lose faith in Washington's insiders and a desperate nation looked for a new face to take the lead. Once he secured his parties nomination Jimmy jumped out to an early lead in the polls over his opponent incumbent President Gerald R. Ford.

Ford was born in Nebraska in 1913 and was originally named Leslie Lynch King, Jr. His parents divorced and he was raised by his mother and step-father, Gerald R. Ford, whose name he was then given. Gerry, as he was known, was a top student and an excellent football player. Eventually he would receive offers to play professionally but chose to study law at Yale. When World War II broke out he volunteered to serve in the navy and saw combat as an officer in the Pacific.

After the war Gerry ran for Congress on the Republican ticket and won in a landslide. He was repeatedly elected to the office. In 1963 President Johnson appointed Ford to the Warren Commission to investigate the assassination of John F. Kennedy. In 1965 he became the minority leader of the House of Representatives. Then in 1973, following the resignation of Vice President Spiro Agnew, President Nixon asked Gerry, because of his ability to work with Congress and his impeccable reputation, to fill Agnew's position. Then, only nine months later, Nixon resigned the office in order to avoid impeachment proceedings that were brought about by the Watergate scandal and Ford ascended to the Presidency.

One of the first important acts that Ford performed was to grant a pardon to President Nixon for any crimes he may have committed while in the White House. Ford hoped that the pardon would put an end to the "long national nightmare" of Watergate but it only fueled more cynicism towards the government. Some Americans believed that Ford and Nixon had made a deal to allow Ford to become President if he would grant a pardon. In addition, Gerry then had to cope with bringing American involvement in Vietnam to a complete conclusion as well as a rising unemployment rate and an energy crisis.

It was with this vulnerable opponent in the White House that Jimmy hit the campaign trail. Following his nomination Jimmy enjoyed a lead in the polls over Ford by more than 30%. But Gerry was a tenacious and experienced politician and the gap in the polls soon began to narrow. Following a first televised debate Ford had developed momentum and the way he was going he might just win.

Then Jimmy blundered and nearly sealed an election victory for Gerry. Jimmy and his campaign team thought that he might be coming off as a little too straight laced. They thought that perhaps he didn't have broad enough appeal to the liberal members of the Democratic Party. With this in mind Jimmy agreed to be interviewed by reporters from the adult magazine, Playboy. The interview appeared to be going well until near the end when Jimmy was quoted to say:

> Christ said, "I tell you that anyone who looks on a woman with lust has in his heart already committed adultery." I've looked on a lot of women with lust. I've committed adultery in my heart many times. This is something that God recognizes I will do—and I have done it—and God forgives me for it. But that doesn't mean that I condemn someone who not only looks on a woman with lust but who leaves his wife and shacks up with somebody out of wedlock. Christ says, don't consider yourself better than someone else because one guy screws a whole bunch of women while the other guy is loyal to his wife. The guy who's loyal to his wife ought not to be condescending or proud because of the relative degree of sinfulness.

Some thought Jimmy's statement to be creepy and so the race tightened until it was nearly a tie. Jimmy went into the next debate on the defensive. But, then as luck would have it, it was Gerry's turn to blunder.

When asked about the control of Eastern Europe by the Russians Gerry responded, "There is no Soviet domination of Eastern Europe and there never will be under a Ford administration." Many were startled to think that Gerry did not appear to understand the degree of Soviet influence in Europe. Some questioned weather a man with this apparently faulty point of view should be in charge of America's foreign policy.

Jimmy did not necessarily gain in the polls as a result of Gerry's gaff but it did stop his downward trend. Nonetheless, even on election day, November 2, 1976 it was anyone's guess who would win. Finally, it was after 3 a.m. the next morning when Jimmy got the news. He won, he was to be the 39th President of the United States.

CHAPTER VII

ENOUGH ADVENTURE
FOR A LIFETIME

"Work is love made visible"
- Kahlil Gibran (author of The Prophet.)

When Mister Earl died in 1954, a light went out inside Miz Lillian. Despondent, bitter and alone, she felt as if her life had no meaning and she would rather be dead, lying cold and in the ground alongside Mister Earl, than to continue on through life without him. As time went by she found useful employment as a house mother for a fraternity at Auburn University, where she worked for eight and a half years. She then went on to manage a nursing home.

Yet for all of her effort, she never found the fulfillment for which she so desperately yearned. There was still a sorrow in her, a darkness brought on not only by Earl's death but by the lack of a true challenge to her potential. She had much to offer and much to overcome. But as she reached her upper sixties the clock was silently, steadily, ticking away.

She sat alone in her comfortable chair, in the dark, one night in the Pond House and took a long, thoughtful, drag off of her cigarette. The television was on, but at that moment commercials were running. She looked out the window dreamily as the moon glistened over her beloved pond, and a large fish, all silver in the moonlight, leapt high out of the water and quickly splashed back in. She exhaled and raised a glass to her lips to take a sip of her mixed drink.

"Age is no barrier." "Huh! Wha? Age is no barriah ta wha?" A commercial for the Peace Corps was concluding, and suddenly a light flashed back on inside of her. She was instantly inspired. Age is no barrier to join the Peace Corps. The answer came to her right there and right then.

The Peace Corps was created by way of the orders of President John F. Kennedy in 1961. Volunteer American citizens would work to promote world peace and friendship by offering their qualified services to interested countries.

There wasn't any doubt that she had the talent to help. She had studied nursing and worked for years in and around Plains. She was tireless in her dedication to all the people of her community, both black and white.

She would not hesitate to help a black family that needed medical assistance, more often than not taking no payment for her services. Although she worked with black people, she was not ostracized by her neighbors, some of whom were extremely racist. They recognized that someone had to help, and Miz Lillian was the one who was most capable and most willing.

Her attitude stemmed from her relationship with her father. She worshiped him. James, known as Jim Jack, was a liberal man especially when it came to the matter of race. He was a friend to white people and to black, all the same. He didn't talk about his attitude because it just came as second nature to him. As a child Lillian observed her father's behavior and often watched him sit down and eat his meal with black people. She admired his convictions and embraced them for herself.

With Mister Earl it was a different story. He did not believe in integration. He thought that segregation was best for both black and white people. Earl was very much a man of his time, whereas Lillian represented the changing South, the South of the future. Although Earl did not believe in integration, he did not stop Lillian from practicing her beliefs, including welcoming black visitors as they entered the house through the front door and treating black people medically the same as she would white people. Today these acts may not sound like much, but in Miz Lillian's time they were nothing short of radical actions.

But she always had to be careful about her behavior and she had become sick and tired of tip-toeing around the segregationists. She wanted to help others in order to lend greater meaning to her own life.

She mailed in her application, volunteering to serve, and then she had second thoughts, but upon consulting with her children found she had unanimous support from the four, prompting her to enquire, "Are ya'lll so glad ta get rid a me?" And so it was that in 1966, at the age of 68, Miz Lillian joined the Peace Corps.

The required psychiatric evaluation showed that she wanted to serve in a country with dark skinned people to compensate for living a lifetime in a segregated society. She explained, "Ah wanted ta work wit people who were underdawgs."

Human sexuality was part of her three month training program, and her instructor happened to be a black man. She thought, "Lord, folks in Plains would have a fit." Soon she was off to India.

While in India she kept a careful journal of her daily experiences. On Dec 22, 1966 she wrote,

> We are in the Peace Corps, under the Indian government, and working in Family Planning for Godrej Industries. The Godrej Colony is about thirty miles from Bombay. There are no stores here. Godrej is an industrial complex with all types of factories, and they have their own health program, cooking classes, school, gymnasium - everything except white people.

It wasn't long before her medical knowledge came flooding back. She assisted the Doctor in a local clinic by giving hundreds of injections, dressing countless wounds, aiding some patients afflicted with leprosy and assisting in examinations and diagnosis. On occasion she would administer injections to hundreds of children in a single day.

Miz Lillian ignored the caste system and treated everyone alike, just as she had done in segregated Georgia. Some of the patients began to think of her as the kindest person that they had ever known. She wrote in her journal that she became sick to her stomach when she would see the small children naked and shivering come to the clinic suffering from pneumonia.

Seeing tiny babies with no food and no clothes on a daily basis made her push all the harder for greater birth control. There was significant resistance to family planning because it was believed that God opposed it. Yet in one day she assisted in performing over thirty vasectomies.

She regularly channeled any frustrations or anger she had in her into trying to do more good and working harder than ever. She noted, "Each day, my tasks are heavier - I am increasingly more tired, but go to bed early and kind of recoup my strength."

She developed a deep tan as time went on. She began to think that she was turning "dark to match my friends." She wondered what it would be like when she returned to Plains and expressed her undying love for people of color.

After a while material things began to lose all meaning. At one point she purchased a beautiful cashmere shawl. On a freezing cold day she wore the shawl to the clinic. She spied a patient shivering with pneumonia and, having no blankets, she took off the shawl and wrapped him in it.

She wrote, "I didn't dream that in this remote corner of the world, so far away from the people and material things that I had always considered so necessary, I would discover what life is really all about, sharing yourself with others - and accepting their love for you is the most precious gift of all."

Only one material thing never ceased to lose its value to her. Books. Unfortunately, there was a dearth of reading material. She tried to adjust to this fact but suffered regularly. Finally, one day, a crate arrived from the Peace Corps with over one hundred paperback books in it. Although exhausted, she read deep into the night and then arose early the next morning to read some more.

She sat and read in her apartment with the windows open, and little birds would fly in, around, and out of the room all day long. Once she sat reading Death of a President about John F. Kennedy's assassination when a lark flew in and stood singing his heart out just a few inches from her. The small bird, brown and white, seemed to be singing to her as he cocked his head and looked directly at her. She returned to her book, and tears welled up in her eyes as she read about the loss of this young American President.

The local people could often be kind to her. Mr. Vinod, the gardener would bring her flowers and vegetables. In return she taught his daughter, Madhavi, seven years old, how to read and write, in English.

She managed living through her first monsoon. The wind at seventy miles an hour was so incredibly powerful that she thought it sounded as if a large jet plane was landing on the roof. It took some getting used to, but she learned to love the incessant rain.

As time went on she, naturally, missed home very badly. When she started losing weight her family sent her as much food as the Peace Corps would allow and that could survive the postal trip, only to be given away to the poor and the ill.

She sat feeling terribly homesick while she looked at family pictures she had decorating the edges of her mirror. All of the faces in the pictures were smiling broadly at her, and she tried gamely to smile back.

She wrote every week and occasionally received happy news from home in return. For instance, Jimmy reported that Rosalynn was going to have another baby. She had been so down, and then she read the letter, and her morale shot way up again. Seven months later she was further elated by the news that a daughter, Amy, was born.

The newspapers kept her up to date on the dynamic happenings from the rapidly changing America. She was delighted to learn that Bobby Kennedy was going to run for President. Then less than three weeks later she was badly shaken by the news of the assassination of Dr. Martin Luther King, Jr.

In early June she sat up late one night reading when a single lark, brown and white, flew into her room and began to sing... to her! The next day her heart was broken when she learned that Robert Kennedy had been shot and later died. Her friends and colleagues tried to assuage her pain, but no one could reach her. Finally, after all that she had seen, she completely lost control and appeared inconsolable. On her day off she just sat all alone, in her nightgown, completely despondent. Now, she could only think about going home.

But by mid-August she began to snap out of it. She turned seventy years old and started to think of "where I am, and what I'm doing, and why." She wrote, "If I had one wish for my children, it would be that each of you would dare to do the things and reach for goals in your own lives that have meaning for you as individuals, doing as much as you can for everybody, but not worrying if you don't please everyone."

And now she felt that she had enough adventure for a lifetime. She had never worked so hard in her entire life and never loved it more than she had during those two years. She thought that she had done a little to help the people of India, but that they had done much, much more for her. Her experiences had brought greater value to her than anything else she had ever done in her entire life.

She returned home to Plains a complete human being.

Jimmy's drawing of his childhood home in Archery, Georgia.
*"He nearly flew back down the hall, across the porch and out
the door to his waiting buddy who bellowed, 'Le's go!'."*

15 year old Jimmy at an FFA summer camp.
*"Shirtless and barefoot as usual, he is
wearing an old pair of blue jeans."*

"Daddy sat, aloof, in his chair...reading the newspaper by the light of the kerosene lamp."

"... he dashed briskly up the eight steps to the front door of the large red brick school building with the massive white columns in front."

Teenage Rosalynn Smith.
*"Despite everything, she managed to graduate
from Plains High School as valedictorian."*

Jimmy at Annapolis.
*"Suddenly, one day, she noticed a picture
hanging on the wall in Ruth's room."*

Jimmy's famous toothy grin and peanut farmer
notoriety are manifested in this Plains sculpture.
*"Jimmy had a huge smile on his face, his large
teeth glistening in the Georgia sunlight."*

New York politician Bella Abzug with Jimmy in
the Saint Patrick's Day Parade in 1976.
"He seemed to have come out of nowhere."

Billy Carter.

"Then, in 1972, he purchased a gas station, not far from the warehouse, where he could hang out with his many friends, drink beer and play the clown."

Rosalynn, Jimmy and Amy at the high point of his political career.
"Finally it was 3 a.m. the next morning when Jimmy got the news.
He won, he was to be the 39th President of the United States."

Jimmy with one of his heroes Admiral Hyman
Rickover and Energy Secretary Dr. James
R. Schlesinger.

*"Jimmy realized right away that the nation's dependency on
foreign oil was dangerously high at almost 50% of our demand..."*

Amy and Mary Fitzpatrick.

*"It was undoubtedly strange that Miss Fitzpatrick held this
trusted position inasmuch as she was a convicted murderer."*

Prime Minister Menachem Begin, Jimmy
and President Anwar al-Sadat.
*"After just a few days it became apparent that if his plan stood
any chance of succeeding the two men could not meet together."*

Jimmy and Miz Lillian in the White House.
"Capitalizing on her popularity Jimmy began
asking her to help with some official events."

Senator Ted Kennedy and Jimmy meeting in the Oval Office.
"Even his own Democratic Party was divided."

Amy, Rosalynn and Jimmy at the low point of his political career.
*"There was nothing left for him to do now
except to go home...home to Plains."*

Billy's resting place.
"Now, all he needed, all he wanted, was a
little time to make a real difference."

Abbie Hoffman and Amy.
"Amy, Hoffman and fifty eight others were
arrested for various charges including trespassing,
disorderly conduct and obstructing justice."

Jimmy at the Maranatha Baptist Church.
"Any Sunday that he is in Plains you can find him here
speaking about the lessons of the 'good book'."

Jimmy at a recent book signing.
"He enjoys considerable success as an author,
having written nearly thirty books that, for the
most part, have been well received."

"By far, my best years are those Ah'm enjoying
right now, since Rosalynn and Ah left the
White House."

CHAPTER VIII

THY SEA IS SO GREAT

"Far better it is to dare mighty things, to win glorious triumphs even though checkered by failure, than to rank with those poor spirits who neither enjoy nor suffer much because they live in the gray twilight that knows neither victory nor defeat." – Theodore Roosevelt (Naturalist, author, big game hunter and President of the United States.)

After taking the oath of office and addressing the thousands on hand and the millions watching on televisions and listening on radios, Jimmy surprised everyone when instead of riding in a limousine, he began to walk the distance of the inaugural parade from the Capitol building to his new home, the White House. Surrounded by his family, holding Rosalynn's hand, he briskly strode down the avenue waving and smiling to the tens of thousands of Americans who came to see their brand new, open and honest President.

One of his first important acts as President took place on his second day in office when he was to daringly grant amnesty to thousands of men who had evaded the draft during the Vietnam War. It was his hope that it would help to bring an end to the divisiveness that had taken place in America as a result of the war. The act angered some veteran groups and pleased others, and so the war remained a divisive issue.

Jimmy realized right away that the nation's dependency on foreign oil was dangerously high at almost 50% of our demand and steadily rising. In addition, Americans were consuming more energy than ever before. As the cost of imported oil continued to increase, then prices, in general, correspondingly rose. If it cost more because of higher gas prices, for instance, for a truck to deliver a load of fruit to market, then fruit prices would also rise.

Jimmy recognized the necessity of managing our limited resources with greater efficiency and, therefore, instituted a new cabinet seat called the Department of Energy and named Dr. James R. Schlesinger to head the post.

He encouraged Americans to reduce daily energy consumption in many small ways, for example, by turning down their thermostats. He had solar panels installed on the White House roof and a wood burning stove placed in the family living quarters. In February, 1977, he addressed the nation for the first of five times on the energy problem. He wrote in his address, "The amount of energy being wasted which could be saved is greater than the total energy that we are importing from foreign countries...we will emphasize research on solar energy and other renewable energy sources."

Jimmy successfully introduced legislation that, among other things: encouraged car pooling and gasohol production through tax incentives; strongly encouraged solar-power development as well as tax incentives for the installation of solar units in homes and other buildings; offered the first incentives to produce corn-based ethanol; and penalized the manufacturers of gas-guzzling automobiles.

Jimmy signed into law legislation that established a "Superfund"--that is, "a system of insurance premiums collected from the chemical industry to clean up toxic wastes." It was his hope that this fund would significantly reduce the risk that toxic waste sites presented to the well-being of millions of Americans.

As an environmentalist, Carter's crowning achievement was his Alaska Interest Lands Conservation Act, which he signed into law in December, 1980. The Secretary of the Interior during the Carter Administration, Cecil Andrus, wrote,

> Carter managed to leave behind a legacy of volcanic craters, alpine lakes, ancient forests, tundras needed by grizzly bears, and federal land managers who weren't devoted only to drilling, digging up, and cutting down the great resources of America's forty-ninth state.

The 103 million acres of Alaska, more than 25 percent of the State, set aside as a national park land was the largest land conservation initiative in the history of the United States. Cecil Andrus would further note that, "Jimmy Carter was, with Theodore Roosevelt, one of the two most committed conservationists ever to occupy the Oval Office."

Jimmy continued to keep in touch with nature all of the time that he was in the White House. When the demands of office were beginning to get the better of him, he would board the presidential helicopter and fly off to the chief executives retreat, known as Camp David, in Maryland. The members of the press would think him safely ensconced behind the camp gates when his helicopter would secretly take off again. Jimmy and Rosalynn would be flown to a secluded creek in Pennsylvania where they would peacefully fish for a couple of days.

He had some successes in foreign policy, too, establishing, for example, full diplomatic relations with the People's Republic of China, completing negotiations with the Soviet Union on a nuclear arms limitation treaty (SALT II) and getting Congressional approval for a Panama Canal Treaty wherein the canal was eventually handed over to the government of Panama. He became a champion of human rights around the globe.

By the end of his time in office he was able to significantly reduce the budget deficit, and the nation saw almost eight million new jobs created. Despite his best efforts, however, inflation rose to dizzying heights, as did interest rates. And although the overall unemployment rate was relatively low, there were places in the country where it was inordinately high, sometimes as much as 18%.

There were serious problems involving foreign policy, as well. In Iran, militant students stormed and took over the U.S. embassy in the capitol city of Tehran in November, 1979. Americans were held captive, and nothing that Jimmy could do would secure their release.

The Soviet Union invaded Afghanistan on Christmas Eve, 1979 increasing tensions between the Super Powers. Jimmy responded by suspending plans to ratify the SALT II agreement, issuing economic sanctions, and boycotting the Olympics that were to be held in Russia.

Because the Russians had the audacity to invade Afghanistan and the Iranians took over the American Embassy, many people began to think that Jimmy was seen as weak by our foreign adversaries. Americans seemed to lose confidence in him, and it became clear to all when his popularity waned in opinion polls.

Even his own Democratic Party was divided. The Liberal branch of the party saw Jimmy's election as an opportunity to re-invigorate Lyndon Johnson's Great Society programs, while Jimmy was more interested in cutting spending and balancing the budget. This rift led to a challenger to his Presidency from within.

Ted Kennedy was the youngest of Rose and Joe Kennedy's children. His godfather was none other than his older brother and future President, John F. Kennedy, known familiarly as "Jack". Jack petitioned to have his baby brother named George Washington Kennedy since he was born on Washington's 200th Birthday, but instead he was named after Joe's assistant, Edward Moore, and nicknamed Ted.

He was raised in an extraordinarily privileged environment of great wealth, but he knew his share of tragedy, inasmuch as his brother and sister were both killed, Joe in WWII in 1944 and Kathleen in 1948 in an airplane crash.

Ted was an average student in school and a good football player. Like his father and brothers before him, he attended Harvard where he continued to play football. He was caught cheating on a Spanish exam and was expelled, but was told that he could reapply in the future if he exhibited good behavior.

He enlisted in the Army and served as an MP in France. He was discharged as a Private First Class. Ted returned to Harvard a better student, and he also returned to its football team at 6'2" and weighing 200 pounds. He graduated in 1956 with a degree in History and Government. He then attended the University of Virginia School of Law. He managed Jack's re-election campaign to the Senate. He married soon after he graduated from law school.

When Jack ran for President, Ted managed the campaign in the Western States. After Jack won the election his Senate seat was vacated, and Ted ran to fill it. He too won and entered the Senate at the minimum age of 30.

On November 22, 1963, Ted was quietly presiding over the Senate, busily signing correspondence as a dull debate droned on. Suddenly, he heard a shout from the lobby. He was called to the side and told that Jack had been shot. Within an hour he learned that his beloved brother was dead.

Then, in June, 1964 while a passenger in a private jet flying from Washington to Massachusetts, his plane crashed killing one of his assistants and the pilot. He was seriously injured and would suffer from severe back pain for the rest of his life. While convalescing in the hospital he was overwhelmingly re-elected to the Senate.

Ted returned and became an important voice in the Upper House. In 1968 his surviving brother, Bobby, decided to run for President, and Ted helped rally support for him. He was in California in June, 1968, when Bobby too was shot down and killed. Ted was absolutely devastated. Fighting back tears he delivered an eloquent eulogy at St. Patrick's Cathedral in New York City.

Now, at only 36, he was, in effect, the patriarch of the family and the stand-in father for 13 nephews and nieces. Ted was seen by many as the natural opponent to Richard Nixon in '72. But the physical pain from the plane crash, the psychological agony caused by the loss of his brothers and sister, and the constant fear of being shot one day drove him to self medicate with alcohol.

In July, 1969 he threw a party for a group of women who had worked on his brother's campaign the year before. He left the party in Martha's Vineyard's Chappaquiddick Island with Mary Jo Kopechne, 28, and accidentally drove off a bridge into a tidal channel. The car flipped in the water, but he managed to escape as it sunk. He dove seven or eight times to try and rescue Mary Jo but failed and then fled the scene. He didn't contact the authorities until the next morning. Mary Jo was dead.

He pleaded guilty to leaving the scene of an accident and was given a sentence of two months in jail, suspended. Aside from the questions of character that the accident raised, the scandal seriously damaged his future presidential prospects.

Ted continued to work hard in the Senate, and his image improved in time although the young woman's death continued to haunt him. He became a champion of the liberal agenda in Washington and was America's most famous Democrat - until Jimmy Carter came to town. Teddy and the other Washington liberals saw the election of a Democratic president as an opportunity to push their programs forward and were terribly disappointed by Jimmy's more conservative economic philosophy.

Some predicted that Jimmy would lose if he ran for re-election against Republican Presidential hopeful Ronald Reagan. Ted, sensing vulnerability, finally decided to seek the Democratic nomination for himself in the 1980 presidential election.

He ran a weak campaign. He was handcuffed by his fear of an assassin lurking around every corner and the constant dark cloud over his head brought on by the death of Mary Jo. When interviewed on the news he even stumbled when he tried to answer a simple question like, "Why do you want to be president?"

By the time the convention rolled around Jimmy had many more delegates than were needed for the nomination, but Ted would not quit because he thought he could have the rules altered so that the delegates would be free to change their pledge. The rules were not changed, and Ted finally had to concede defeat. In the end Ted was just too liberal, and the pall cast by his disgraceful behavior at Chappaquiddick could never completely leave his presence.

When Ted and Jimmy appeared together on the stage at the convention in Madison Square Garden, Jimmy was hoping that they could raise one another's hand above their heads in a sign of triumphant unity. That did not happen. Instead, it appeared that Ted was trying to stay away from Jimmy, sending a signal to the country that the party was still divided. This signal really hurt Jimmy's campaign.

The Republican Party did put forth Ronald Reagan as their candidate. Ronald had once been a popular movie star who, following his film career, entered politics and was twice elected Governor of California. Ronald's optimistic, can do attitude and his tendency to speak in grand, sweeping terms stood in sharp contrast to Jimmy's more serious and detail-oriented approach to running the country.

With just a week or so to go before the election, some polls indicated that the race could go either way. Jimmy's team decided that agreeing to a debate would be just what was needed to break into the lead. They thought that Jimmy could show off his amazing knowledge of the myriad challenges that the nation faced. They believed that they could show Ronald to be a dowdy, trigger happy gunslinger who couldn't be trusted with caring for America's nuclear arsenal.

But Ronald did not fumble or lose his cool. In fact, he came off as very much in control. When he encouraged the American people to ask themselves, "Are you better than you were four years ago?" he caused enough doubt in people's minds to swing the polls decisively in his direction.

Not long after the debate Jimmy sat behind his desk in the Oval Office with only the sound of a ticking grandfather clock to break the deep and somber silence. Jimmy glanced over at a plaque that was given to him by Admiral Rickover. It read, "O, God, Thy sea is so great and my boat is so small."

He is resting for a brief moment before returning to his work. Jimmy is now a very, very disappointed man. Eventually, his presidency would be most remembered for two events of which one was seen as a stunning triumph and the other thought to be a sad failure.

CHAPTER IX

A "CHAINSAW" FOR CHRISTMAS

"She discusses international issues, including the hostage crisis, almost like an adult." **Jimmy Carter (President of the United States.)**

They had poured in by the thousands. Everyday, especially since Jimmy's nomination for the Presidency, more and more people made their way to Plains. Eight year old Amy Carter shrewdly sensed an opportunity. She asked her two friends, neighbors John and Sidney, if they wanted to make some money. Would they be willing to work with her?

The three stacked up cardboard boxes for their stand and then charged five cents for a cup of ice cold lemonade. It wasn't long before they realized that it cost more than five cents per each drink served for lemons, cups, sugar and ice. And so, with great industry, they rebuilt their stand from wood and increased their price to ten cents. For fifteen cents one could have a picture taken with Amy too. One day the three friends earned $23.

That same year she was lucky enough to go to New York City with her father and mother while Jimmy was nominated to run for President as the Democratic Party candidate. She went to Central Park and climbed all over the statues of Alice in Wonderland and Hans Christian Anderson. She went to the zoo where she purchased a lemon ice and saw the baby gorilla, Patty Cake. She fed peanuts to the other animals.

Then, while walking back to the Americana Hotel, she noticed a playground near the children's zoo and asked her mother if she could stop there. She joined about fifteen little black children from the Sheltering Arms Day Camp on the slides, swings and monkey bars.

For all of the fun things she saw and did while she was in New York, there was one thing that she wanted to do the most, and that was to go home to Plains and climb trees. In fact, a number of observers thought her quite bored with the whole New York experience. She did not look forward to going to the White House. She loved Plains because it was small and she knew everyone there. Often appearing to be introspective and aloof, Amy, in fact, even hoped that Jimmy would lose the election.

Yet she could be fairly passionate about certain political beliefs. She cried, for example, when her father told her that Walter Mondale was to be his Vice Presidential running mate and not the exciting astronaut hero turned politician, John Glenn.

Regardless of her feelings, her blond hair, bespectacled blue eyes, toothy grin and freckled face endeared her to millions of Americans.

On Inauguration Day Amy, sitting next to Rosalynn, smiled only a little and then even yawned once when Jimmy took the oath of office. Later, during the inaugural parade, she got out of the car and ran and skipped up to her parents who were walking down the middle of Pennsylvania Avenue. She was responsible for the parade stopping twice, once when she fastened a button and another time when she tied a bootlace.

After the inaugural parade Amy ran around on the White House lawn with her nursemaid. Mary Fitzpatrick had been Amy's nursemaid while Jimmy was Governor. It was undoubtedly strange that Miss Fitzpatrick held this trusted position inasmuch as she was a convicted murderer who had been sentenced to life in prison.

As a visitor to a small South Georgia town Mary had been involved in a street fight in 1970 during which a man she had never seen before had been shot and killed. Without adequate legal counsel, she was convicted of murder, and although some were convinced that she was innocent, she was serving out a life sentence.

It was a common practice in the South to assign prisoners to work details in public facilities, including the governor's mansion. Mary Fitzpatrick, then, became Amy's nursemaid and close friend.

After Jimmy was elected President he contacted the Georgia Pardon and Parole Board and asked if Mary might be allowed to come to Washington to take care of Amy. She would be paid as a regular employee, and Jimmy and Rosalynn would be responsible for her good behavior. The board agreed to those terms.

She lived in a small room on the third floor of the White House and performed her duties in an exemplary manner. Mary proved to be of special help during the times when both Rosalynn and Jimmy had to be away from home. There was some criticism about having a criminal in the White House, but it didn't matter.

When Jimmy was elected it was decided that Amy would go to public school as a statement of principle. The Stevens School, a building with seven rooms, was close to the White House, built in 1868 for the children of freed slaves and was named after anti-slavery Congressman Thaddeus Stevens.

It was the first school for black children in Washington, D.C. Stevens had 215 pupils, of whom about 60% were black, 30% oriental or hispanic, and 10% white. Some of the students were children of foreign diplomats and servants assigned to Washington. Amy's classmates were from Pakistan, Romania, and India, among other places.

Upon enrolling in the fourth grade, Amy became the first child of an incumbent president to study in a public classroom since Theodore Roosevelt's son, Quentin. On her first day of school she arrived ten minutes late. The five block trip from the White House took a half hour, and Mrs. Carter had calculated that the trip would take twenty minutes. Amy walked into her new classroom carrying a blue canvas tote bag with a drawing of "Snoopy" the dog printed on it.

Amy told Jimmy her views of the public school system in the District of Columbia and discussed the lives of her classmates, some of them children of the servants in foreign embassies.

Meanwhile, the Carters relaxed while watching Amy play tag or hide and seek in the hallowed halls of the White House and roller skate under the arcade and along the paths. Due to her great popularity Amy was assigned many duties. Once she was asked to accept a baby elephant on behalf of the children of the United States at the National Zoo. The elephant was a gift from Sri Lanka and named "Shanti." On another occasion Amy accepted two reindeer from Finland, also a gift to the National Zoo.

She performed in the East Room of the White House with stage and screen star Helen Hayes before 430 children from embassies from all over the world in a brief play called "The Littlest Clown." Hayes hugged her and proclaimed her to be "a real trouper."

Sometimes the demands on the small girl proved to be more than she was equipped to handle. Once when she was scheduled to unveil a poster for the new Department of Education, everyone waited and looked at their watches. Amy was in her room getting ready and, by now, she should have returned. When Rosalynn went to check on her she found her sound asleep in the bathtub.

Amy would sit between her parents at state dinners for people like the President of Mexico, Jose Lopez Portillo, and for Prime Minister Pierre Trudeau of Canada. She shocked social observers by reading at the table. Jimmy explained that his whole family read at the table, and they never considered it to be ill mannered.

As first daughter she occasionally got to travel to exotic places. She went with her parents on Air Force One to South America and Nigeria, for instance. Protecting her parents during an economic summit in Venice, the Secret Service became alarmed by the possibility of assassination attempts by a terrorist gang called the Red Brigade. They requested that the First Lady and Amy wear bulletproof vests. The vests were hot and bulky, and they had to wear jackets to disguise them. Everyone around kept asking why they were wearing coats, and Rosalynn made up weak excuses. During a visit to a glass blowing plant Rosalynn nearly suffocated from the heat, but Amy took it all without complaint.

When Radio City Music Hall was in financial trouble, Amy and her schoolmates took a bus to New York City to visit the famous theater. She was disturbed by the many photographers, reporters and television crews who followed her around. "Let 'em take pictures of my parents," she was heard to say.

Amy had a treehouse on the edge of the White House South lawn. It rested on four posts next to a forty foot sprawling silver cedar. The design of the tree house was suggested by Jimmy. It was a refuge where she even spent a night with her friend, Mary Fitzpatrick, and her dog Grits. On one occasion, at least, Jimmy climbed up to check out this very basic getaway first hand.

It wasn't long before The White House was receiving 3,000 to 4,000 letters a week from elementary school children, many of them addressed to Amy, to learn about the home of the President and his family. A 12 page booklet that answered questions about the White House was soon created. It featured pictures of Amy, including one of her sitting on her father's lap in the Oval Office and one of her sitting on the stairs to the White House entrance hall.

Somehow, a rumor started that Amy wanted a chainsaw for Christmas. A manufacturer rushed her a red, white and blue chain saw as a present. The gift caused confusion among the White House staff. When asked why she wanted a chainsaw, Amy clarified that it was all a misunderstanding, she wanted a train set, not a chainsaw.

In June, 1978, the Carter's decided to transfer Amy from the Stevens School to the Hardy Middle School near some of Washington's most expensive homes. She would begin the sixth grade there in the fall of 1978.

In Christmas 1979 Amy lit the National Tree in Washington, D.C. The tree was only partially lit because of the fifty hostages being held in the embassy in Iran. Fifty small trees lit up in commemoration of the hostages, and a star shaped cluster of lights lit up on top of the main tree, a thirty foot blue spruce.

When Jimmy ran for re-election, Amy's elder sibling Chip, while on the campaign trail, always introduced himself as "Amy's brother," a line that never failed to produce laughter and charm the audience.

In October when Jimmy met his opponent Ronald Reagan in the debate, Jimmy told millions of Americans that he had asked his daughter Amy what the biggest problem in the world was, and she told him that it was nuclear weaponry. Jimmy was roundly ridiculed.

He had written in his diary on October 26, 1980,

I talked to Amy on the phone about the upcoming debate. I won't see her again for about a week. She said that the atomic bomb was the most important issue, and we had a discussion about what a kiloton was, what a megaton was. She discusses international issues, including the hostage crisis, almost like an adult.

Jimmy's statement during the debate about Amy's concern over nuclear weapons made her "the most famous anti-nuclear advocate in America because of the ridicule it aroused from Governor Reagan and the news reporters."

Jimmy's comments regarding his twelve year old daughter did not have the effect for which he had hoped. On the contrary, it made Jimmy look to many as naive and silly.

Amy had made many friends while in the White House and adjusted to her new life in D.C. when suddenly it would be all over.

CHAPTER X

"MY FRIEND JIMMY"

"A little courtesy all around helps to smooth out the most complicated problems." - James Hilton (Author of Lost Horizon.)

In 1948, 1956, 1967 and again in 1973 Egypt and Israel went to war with one another. These wars resulted in the death of a total of over 20,000 Egyptian and Israeli soldiers. Three leaders had determined that they would put a stop to this cycle of violence. The differences and animosities between the two countries were so great, however, that chances of achieving this goal were, at best, extremely slim.

Anwar al-Sadat was born in 1918, about 40 miles north of Cairo, Egypt. He was one of thirteen children. His father was a civil servant who did not earn much money. Anwar was not a good student because he was, what his teachers called, a daydreamer.

When Anwar was a boy Egypt was a Protectorate, that is to say, under the control of Great Britain. He became impressed with Nazi dictator Adolph Hitler because of his opposition to the British. When he was in high school his family moved to Cairo. Once he was in the big city he became active in protesting the British presence by joining in demonstrations.

Then, in 1936, he was accepted into a military academy where he studied Egyptian history and learned about warfare. Around this time he got married. It was an arranged marriage. Within a few years he was the father of three daughters and unhappy with his wife.

After he graduated from the academy Anwar was stationed with Gamal Abdel Nasser. Along with Nasser and a few others he helped to form the Free Officers Organization, a revolutionary group that wanted to rid Egypt of King Farouk, whom they saw as England's puppet, and end their protectorate status. Anwar ended up in prison for trying to get the Germans to help drive the British out of Egypt.

Once released from prison, after three years, he divorced, met a young woman named Jihan, and eventually married her. Soon he joined up with Nasser again. While he had been incarcerated the revolutionary movement had grown considerably. The Free Officers led the Egyptian Revolution of 1952, in which Anwar participated, and they staged a successful coup forcing the King into exile. Nasser gained control and became Egypt's President. By 1964 Anwar rose to the position of Vice President. Then, in September, 1970 Nasser died. Anwar then ascended to the Presidency.

In 1973 he led a war against Israel in an effort to regain land lost in a previous war. Among those killed were his brother, Atef. Although Anwar met with limited success he was hailed by Arabs for what they saw as his valiant efforts.

Anwar ultimately grew sick of waging one war after another with his neighbor. In 1977 he pledged to go anywhere to secure peace with Israel and, true to his word, accepted an invitation by the Israelis and spoke to the Knesset in an effort at reconciliation. One day while sitting in his office his secretary stepped in and said, "A phone call, sir, it's The White House."

Born in 1913 in Brest-Litovsk, part of the Russian Empire in what is today the Republic of Belarus, Menachem Begin was one of three children of Orthodox Jewish parents. Like most of the other Jews there the family lived in poverty and under the incessant threat of violent anti-semites.

By the time he was 12 he embraced Zionism, the idea that Jews should return to their homeland and enjoy sovereignty in Israel. By 1938 he was an important leader in the Zionist movement in Eastern Europe. In 1939 he met Aliza Arnold, and after a whirlwind courtship of one month, he married her. The two would go on to have three children.

Menachem was arrested by Joseph Stalin's police force in 1940 for his political activism and was sent to a Siberian prison. After his release in 1942 he made his way to Palestine, then under British control. During World War II he lost his father, mother, and brother, Herzl, in the holocaust.

Menachem joined an anti-British underground military unit and contributed to the overthrow of the imperialist authorities through violent means. He helped, for instance, to organize the bombing of British headquarters in the King David Hotel in Jerusalem where over 90 people were killed and 45 injured. He kept up his resistance until 1948 when the State of Israel was at last officially established.

By the mid-1960's Menachem gained cabinet status in the Israeli government. His continued extreme work in the interest of his beloved Israel caused him to attain the position of Prime Minister in 1977. In December, 1977 he courageously traveled to Egypt to meet with Anwar where the two discussed the possibility of a permanent peace between the two countries. Then soon after, while sitting at his desk a voice on his intercom said, "Washington, D.C. is on the line."

Jimmy recognized the importance that peace in the Middle East held for the security of the United States. The Soviet Union could capitalize on the instability caused by war and make an attempt at imperializing the region. Further, Israel was our ally and as such America had an obligation to support them in their quest for peace. Besides, the U.S. was to a significant degree dependent on the oil that came from the region and for that reason a stable Mid East would help to ensure a steady flow of the "black gold."

With these motives and with, in mind, the Biblical missive, "Blessed are the peacemakers for they shall be the children of God," Jimmy invited Anwar and Menachem to Camp David to do what had not been possible since the birth of Israel: to negotiate a permanent peace with an Arabic country. These two nations had waged no fewer than four bloody wars in less than thirty years, fueling an intense hatred.

Camp David, in the mountains of Maryland, had been a Presidential getaway since the days of Franklin Roosevelt. F.D.R. choose this idyllic spot, originally built by WPA workers as a campground for federal employees, to escape the incredible stress of Washington, D.C. F.D.R.'s health was poor even before World War II broke out, but doctors, alarmed by the enormous strain that the war put on the president, insisted that he find a safe and secure place to get away. F.D.R. christened the place the U.S.S. Shangri La after the mythical utopia of James Hilton's novel, Lost Horizon.

In the 1950's President Eisenhower renamed the spot Camp David in honor of his grandson. Presidents Kennedy, Johnson, Nixon and Ford all made good use of the retreat, with Nixon adding new buildings with modern conveniences. All these men held important meetings there and welcomed important guests, but the meeting that Jimmy planned was positively historic.

When it came time for the summit Jimmy was beyond well prepared, having learned hundreds of tiny details about the Middle East. But it wasn't long after the arrival of these two bitter enemies that he realized he had made a mistake. He thought he could just put the two into a room, and that with him acting as mediator, they would iron out their differences. After just a few days it became apparent that if his plan stood any chance of succeeding, the two men could not meet together. When they were in the same room it wouldn't be long before the discussion for a foundation for peace turned into a hate filled argument.

And so he realized that if this summit were to come to anything he had to separate the two antagonists and work as the go between. He and his staff drafted a proposal for peace. When he could, Jimmy would wander into the forest alone to think and to pray. He was at home in the woods where he could clear his mind and regain his strength.

Then he began his shuttle diplomacy. First he would visit Menachem's cabin and negotiate the details with him, and then he'd go to Anwar's cabin and try to hammer out the agreement there - back and forth until on the tenth day there was a crisis. Anwar had had enough. He didn't think that Menachem was ever going to fully cooperate, and so he packed his bags and was ready to leave.

Jimmy was shocked and feared that all of their efforts would be for nothing. Since the beginning of the summit he had worn casual attire, but now he put on his suit and tie and went to meet Anwar in possession of all the dignity, power and prestige of the President of the United States. He appealed to Anwar's sense of decency and responsibility and implored him to stay just a little longer. Finally, he relented. "All right, my friend Jimmy, I'll stay."

But Jimmy wasn't out of the woods yet. Soon after Anwar's threat to leave, Menachem also said that he was fed up, was throwing in the towel and going home. Jimmy took a more subtle approach with Menachem. He took out photographs of the three of them and autographed each one, personalizing them to Menachem's grandchildren. After all, this is what the summit was about, in the end, securing peace for future generations. Because Menachem loved his grandchildren so much, this gesture melted his heart and, he too, consented to stay.

After thirteen intense days an agreement was at last reached. Among the most important points agreed upon were that Egypt and Israel within months would sign a formal peace treaty and establish diplomatic relations. Jimmy had accomplished the impossible!

Menachem and Anwar returned home to their respective countries and secured the approval of the Cabinet in Egypt and the Knesset in Israel. Then in March, 1979 the two men returned to the United States and this time met Jimmy at the White House, where they signed a formal peace treaty vowing to never go to war with each other again.

It was a great moment for Anwar and Menachem. It was, perhaps, the high water mark of Jimmy's Presidency, but as high he had gone he was soon to experience a low to match. He had struggled with the problems of Egypt and Israel and ultimately found the solution, but before long he would be faced with a problem of equal proportions, and however hard he tried, he would not be able to solve the dilemma. He would be made to appear weak and ineffectual at the hands of a two-bit dictator.

CHAPTER XI

A NATIONAL JOKE

"An intelligent hell would be better than a stupid paradise." Victor Hugo (Author.)

Although Billy continued to drink, heavily, he took his work at the warehouse very seriously and was never known to drink during working hours. His frustration was too great to stifle, however, and so after work he would far more often than not get good and drunk.

He was known, sometimes, to turn very violent. He put his fist through windows, beat his son with a belt, on one occasion tore the telephone from the wall and threw it out the window, and he would sometimes enter into roaring uncontrollable fits of profanity.

He could also be icily cruel. Once, when his daughter, Kim, was 16 she asked if she could get her ears pierced and he said, "No." When she started to cry he just sat up and laughed in her face. She was convinced that he was completely drunk. He was a further embarrassment when he appeared at a high school basketball game so drunk that he fell down some steps in front of Kim and her friends.

Often he promised to be home for some special occasion for the kids; birthdays or holidays, for example, but he never was. He was supposed to escort his daughter Marle at her high school when she was chosen as homecoming queen and instead he called, drunk, at the last minute and canceled.

Despite his affliction he continued to work at the warehouse and do a good job. As Jimmy became increasingly successful in politics, and as it began to take up most of his time, Billy became more involved in the family business. Starting in 1971 and for the next six years, Billy's dream of running the warehouse was made real. Sybil replaced Rosalynn as the company bookkeeper, and she and Billy worked well together. Jimmy later wrote, "I realize that his willingness to operate our farms and warehouse has made it possible for me to hold public office."

Then, in 1972, he purchased a gas station, not far from the warehouse, where he could hang out with his many friends, drink beer and play the clown. The gas station was an oasis where he would relax and enjoy himself with story telling, poker playing and dice shooting as part of the regular agenda. He once reported that he won a Corvette while shooting dice. He kept it for two years, he claimed, before selling it for $6,000.

As time went on, drinking became more and more of a preoccupation for him and the gas station was a perfect place to indulge in his obsession. He was comfortable in his little home town, explaining, "Ah don' like ta go anywhere Ah can't get back ta Plains the same nigh."

When Jimmy made his move to the national stage and decided to run for the Presidency in 1976 the press began to arrive in Plains in large numbers and, ever on the look out for a good story, found a sure fire way to get one by visiting Billy's gas station. Billy would welcome the press and answer all of their questions with wit and candor. They drank his beer and laughed at his jokes and observations on the American cultural and political scene.

When Billy was at home he usually did not drink. He spent his leisure time at home watching baseball, reading and sleeping it off on the couch. Because of his public displays of buffoonery few people realized that Billy was a voracious reader, consuming all sorts of books, all the time. He would generally read five or six or even seven books a week. Billy said, "Ah usually wake up in the middle a the nigh and don' driff off agin fer two o three hours. So Ah keep a stack a books by the bed, and every time Ah go up to Atlanta on business Ah buy $30 o $40 worth mo."

As Jimmy achieved one success after another in the primaries, tourists flocked to Plains by the hundreds, and Billy became an oddity for them to behold. He didn't mind, either. He relished the attention and the fact that he had become a national celebrity simply by being himself.

He began to appear in newspapers and on television news everywhere, generally with a can of beer in his hand. He sold 2,000 cases of beer a week and 40 to 50,000 gallons of gasoline a month from his small station. He was the opposite of the strait laced, serious Jimmy, and people by the thousands found him wonderfully amusing.

Jimmy's political team decided to take advantage of this unexpected good fortune and sent Billy out on the campaign trail. He visited bars and taverns and drank with prospective voters, telling them jokes and giving his point of view on the government, all the while reveling in his popularity and fame.

When Jimmy won the general election the whole town went mad. Tens of thousands of people descended upon Plains, and Billy threw a huge party at his home. By the time the evening was over drunken people were asleep in every corner of the house. Most of them were strangers that Billy had welcomed in.

He went to Washington for the inauguration but didn't like the place much. "Ah'm goin' back ta Plains. Ah haf been in dis town one day an Ah've learnt sumpin: one day in Washington is nough."

Billy then decided to run to be the Mayor of Plains. When asked why, he said, "Well, Ah jus wanted ta run agin the establishment." Jimmy said, "Billy hasn't been ta church in twenty years. But if we had a rule that said that people who sell beer couldn't get in, Billy would be the first to try." He lost by four votes - 82 to 78. "It was the anti-drinkin vote that beat me," he complained.

Jimmy had a controlling investment in the Carter family business, and once he was elected, all of his interests were placed in a blind trust. Billy had asked Jimmy if he could buy him out and run the business himself, but he refused, much to Billy's resentment.

Jimmy later explained that he understood that Billy felt that he was capable of running the business successfully, but that Jimmy had serious doubts about that. Jimmy noted that Billy had become "infatuated with celebrity and was spending more and more time on the road, appearing on 'Hee-Haw' and the like. He was also drinking too much, in my opinion."

The warehouse would be taken out of Billy's control, and he became an employee of a faceless company based in Atlanta. With Jimmy out of the picture and the business in the hands of a distant, seemingly uncaring company, the Carter Warehouse soon began to lose money.

Billy couldn't stand playing second fiddle to this monolithic corporate entity, and so after about a year, with the company fast moving downhill, Billy resigned. In order to protect his families privacy he moved out of Plains, about twenty miles away to a brand new huge house on eight acres of land near Buena Vista, Georgia.

Jimmy worried about his brother, "Ah hate to see Billy hurt himself. Ah'm afraid that he might take something that's very attractive while he's the center of media attention, but then in a year or so it would be gone and he won't have any stability in his life."

No doubt Billy cashed in on his new found national celebrity. He appeared on television's hit show Hee Haw a few times, on Hollywood Squares, and on talk-formatted programs like the Phil Donahue Show, Merv Griffin Show, and Tom Snyder Show. He sometimes earned as much as $5,000. an appearance but spent it as fast as it came in. He made personal appearances all over and wallowed in his fame.

Nationally known for his prodigious drinking habit, he was approached by a beer manufacturer with the idea of naming a beer after him. "Billy Beer" made a big splash initially but wasn't very good and failed after a brief stint.

It wasn't long before his drinking began to take a serious toll on him. At first he seemed like a likable wise-cracking yokel, but as his alcoholism took its firmest grip on him, the downward spiral accelerated.

His appearances on television continued, but his character became more and more that of the clown. He seemed to many like a mentally challenged buffoon. Like the Hunchback of Notre Dame, Quasimodo, he was unofficially crowned "King of the Fools." Billy was no longer amusing in a humorous sort of way; instead, he became a pitiful embarrassment to himself and to his family, especially Jimmy.

Chapter XII

CRISIS AND LOSS

"And when you stop and think about it, we were the icons of a crisis. But this whole nation was held hostage." - Army Colonel Chuck Scott (Chief of the Defense Liaison Office in the American Embassy in Tehran, Iran, and himself a hostage.)

It is November, 1979.

Jimmy paces in the early morning chill of the White House garden. His hands are stuffed down inside his pockets with his head thrown back and his eyes looking, searchingly, upward to the cloudy sky as he silently asks Jesus for direction. He is in serious thought and is painfully troubled. Americans have been taken hostage in Iran, and the kidnappers have made seemingly impossible demands for their release.

Some advisors suggested that Jimmy try to meet these demands, while others told him not to negotiate, but instead to order an attack on Tehran. Some even suggested dropping an Atomic Bomb. He stared down at the ground; if only the solution were as easy to find as those ancient arrowheads he discovered in the dirt on Daddy's farm.

Even under normal circumstances he would have faced a tremendous challenge, but to make matters worse, the leader of Iran behaved in an erratic (Jimmy thought "crazy") fashion. There was no reasoning with this man: the Ayatollah Ruhollah Khomeini.

Khomeini was born in 1902. By the time he was six years old he had begun to study the Qur'an and would continue religious study throughout his childhood. As a young man he excelled in his formal education in Islam as well as in philosophy and poetry. It wasn't long before he became one of the top scholars of Shia Islam. His teachings would often tie his religious beliefs to political and social issues. Eventually, he began to be held in the highest regard by many Iranians.

Khomeini hated the Iranian rulership under the Westernizing and anti-clerical Shah.

The Ayatollah believed the Shah was corrupting the morality of the Iranian people and was a puppet of the United States and Israel. He publicly threatened the Shah and proclaimed that he would be overthrown if he didn't change his evil ways and associations. Khomeini was arrested for his comments, which sparked riots throughout Iran for three days. Later, he was jailed for a year and a half and then forced into exile for the next fourteen years.

While in exile he wrote and preached that the laws of God should be enough for man and that the ruler of a country should be directed by clergy and those well versed in Islam. He taught that Islam did not allow for democracy. He detested all of the fundamental principles embraced by the United States: freedom, equality, and separation of Church and State, to name but a few.

While he built his network of enemies of the Shah, opposition to the regime began to steadily grow in Iran. By the late 1970's

Khomeini was the spiritual leader of the anti-Shah movement. In January, 1979, under tremendous pressure from opponents, the Shah fled Iran, and the following month Khomeini triumphantly returned.

He then appointed an interim Prime Minister. Khomeini proclaimed that anyone who disagreed with him or with his Prime Minister disagreed with God. By late March the Shah's Monarchy was replaced by an Islamic government. Opposition newspapers and political parties were banned. By November, 1979 a new constitution of the Islamic republic was adopted. Khomeini was named Supreme Leader.

But the man that he had deposed did not leave the forefront of the minds of revolutionary leaders. Mohammad Reza Shah Pahlavi was born in Tehran in 1919. He was educated in Switzerland and attended a military academy in Iran. He succeeded his father to the throne in 1941. In the early 1950's he met with strong opposition from a nationalist political opponent, Mohammad Mosaddeq.

Mosaddeq wanted to nationalize British Petroleum's oil interests. The Shah would allow international oil companies to benefit from Iranian oil, took a strong anti-communist stand, and was willing to sell oil to Israel. The United States, therefore, covertly helped to restore the Shah to a position of unchallenged control.

As time went on the Shah concentrated more and more power under his singular authority. With the help of his secret police force, the SAVAK, he suppressed any opposition to his rule. Due to his oppressive tactics he eventually reigned over an unhappy populace.

A constantly increasing gap between the ruling elite and the general population caused further alienation.

Through the instigation of people like the Ayatollah, the Shah's government collapsed, and he was forced to flee the country. Recognizing the unstable condition of Iran at this time, Jimmy arranged to have thousands of American citizens working and living in Iran to return home. He did allow some to stay, including a small diplomatic contingent to continue to run the embassy.

Meanwhile, the Shah began to roam the world, a man without a country. He traveled from Egypt, then to Morocco, and then to the Bahamas. But his wanderings were the least of his problems because the Shah was soon diagnosed with cancer and desperately needed top flight medical care or else he would most certainly die. Highly influential friends, like the wealthy banker David Rockefeller and former Secretary of State Henry Kissinger, convinced Jimmy to allow the Shah into the country on a temporary basis for humanitarian reasons, while he received treatment for cancer at the Cornell University Medical Center in New York City.

Following his operation he began a period of convalescence, during which, Iranian revolutionaries believed, he was plotting with the United States to return to power. The Ayatollah had convinced the revolutionaries that America was at the root of all of their problems, and the Shah's presence in New York served to confirm that belief.

Crowds of thousands of protesters had gathered outside the American embassy in Tehran, and as the morning of November 4th went on they became more and more incensed. At last, they began to scale the walls and, rushing into the building, took more than fifty Americans hostage. The kidnappers demanded the return of the Shah and the money he took from the country with him in his exile, as well as trials of the hostages as spies.

Although some of Jimmy's advisors encouraged him to take decisive immediate military action, he realized that an attack on Tehran would almost certainly result in the killing of the hostages and perhaps thousands of innocent civilians. Jimmy quickly became obsessed with saving the hostages. He would lie awake late at night trying to think of different things that he could do to facilitate their immediate release.

He began to plan a military rescue mission in case negotiations proved fruitless. He wanted it to be "quick, incisive, surgical, no loss of American lives, not involve any other country, minimal suffering of the Iranian people themselves, ... sure of success, and unpredictable."

He decided to put pressure on the Iranians to give him an advantage in the negotiations. One of the first things he did was to order the United States to discontinue all oil purchases from Iran. Then Jimmy looked into the legal possibility of freezing all of Iran's assets in American banks. That would tie up twelve billion of their badly needed dollars. The Iranian assets were soon frozen, and there was support around the world for his ordering the cessation of purchasing Iran's oil.

With the beginning of the 1980 presidential campaign now approaching, Jimmy had a decision to make. Should he continue with his normal campaign schedule or stay in Washington and focus all of his energy on the Iranian crisis and other international conflicts, like the invasion of Afghanistan by the Soviet Union? He decided that the most responsible thing to do was to stay in Washington to try and solve these important problems.

The whole nation then turned its attention to the Iranian hostage crisis. It became something of an American obsession. President Carter did not completely illuminate the national Christmas tree as a sort of symbol of our solidarity with the hostages. Hundreds of thousands of people around the country tied yellow ribbons around trees as an outward sign of their concern for the men and women held in Tehran.

In January, 1980 United Nations Secretary General Kurt Waldheim went to Iran to see if he could negotiate the hostages' release. When he returned to the United States to report to Carter on his trip, he was a man in deep despair. He said that the Iranians were in a complete state of chaos. He was under the impression that the terrorists were in control.

The public opinion polls continued to show support for Jimmy; however, the American people began to demonstrate serious signs of discontent as the weeks passed because of "our seeming impotence in dealing with international crisis." Jimmy was beginning to face increased pressure to take conclusive military action.

There were problems, however, it appeared clear to Jimmy and his advisors that the elected officials of the new government of Iran wanted the hostages released. The Ayatollah Khomeini, a man who in Jimmy's estimation appeared to be mentally unstable, did not want their release, and he was, ultimately, calling the shots. Khomeini then "aborted the resolution of the crisis."

Jimmy's spies in Tehran had kept an eye on the kidnappers, and they reported that less attention was being paid to guard duties. Security would not pose a major problem for anyone determined to force their way onto the compound. The situation was perfect for a rescue operation conducted by a highly skilled, well equipped team of soldiers.

The plan was to fly in eight helicopters under the command of Colonel Charlie Beckwith to a remote desert location about 200 miles Southwest of the embassy site. From there they would fly to Tehran and proceed to free the hostages. The rescue squad was made up of the Army's elite antiterrorist Delta team, men trained by Beckwith himself. It was absolutely essential that there be no leaks. If the kidnappers even suspected an attempt at a rescue, the lives of the hostages would be in serious peril, as would the lives of their would be rescuers.

Problems plagued the mission from the outset. Two of the eight helicopters could not make the journey to the desert location because of an intense sandstorm. One of the six helicopters developed hydraulic difficulties and would not be able to complete the journey. Without six helicopters, the mission could not be carried out.

With daylight fast approaching it became necessary to decide right away if the rescue effort should be aborted or not. The ground commander, Colonel Beckwith, recommended termination, as did the other military leaders. Jimmy then made the heart breaking decision to terminate the mission.

In the great haste to get out of Iran, one of the helicopters, as it was taking off, crashed into an American C130 airplane in the predawn sky. Jimmy was sickened by the disaster and could only wait and pray as the survivors extricated themselves from the desert. Eight men had been killed in the attempt, their burned bodies lying lifeless in the rising sun of the Iranian desert.

The next morning Jimmy went on television and explained to everyone what had happened. He took full responsibility for the failure. The American people responded with support for his efforts.

On May 9th Jimmy went to Arlington National Cemetery for a memorial service for the eight men who died in the rescue attempt. He fretted that he would be repulsed by the loved ones of the men that had been killed. When he and Rosalynn walked into the waiting room where the families had gathered, he was much relieved when they welcomed him with open arms. The families appeared to Jimmy to be uniformly proud that their loved ones had given their lives for their fellow countrymen.

Meanwhile, the Iranians were busily proclaiming victory over the United States, putting photos of bodies and wrecked aircraft on display for the world to see. The hostages were then split up and sent to several locations under heavy guard. They were further moved periodically, making it impossible to know exactly where they all were at any given time.

As the months passed the hostage crisis began to take its toll on Jimmy emotionally and on his popularity. Polls began showing an increasing dissatisfaction with his performance. People felt that Jimmy had not been tough enough in foreign policy, and that this failure exemplified the result of such weakness. Americans were constantly reminded of the crisis on nightly news shows.

The Shah died in July and, coupled with the sanctions Carter had imposed, the Iranians began to express a greater desire to come to the bargaining table. An emissary from the Ayatollah wanted to meet with American officials in Germany. The emissary made more reasonable demands: the return of Iranian assets, the return of the Shah's assets, and a promise that the United States would not interfere in Iranian affairs.

As the Iranian government debated the issue of the hostages, Jimmy campaigned for re-election. There was hope among his campaign staff that he might pull off what Republicans nervously referred to as the "October Surprise," whereby the hostages would be released at the last moment before the November election. With only two days to go, it appeared as if the hostages might be released. Jimmy thought that if this were to happen, he would secure re-election. If not, he would surely lose.

The hostages were not released before election day as Jimmy had hoped. He lost the election and composed an address to the

American people which read, "...I will continue as I have for the last 14 months to work hard and to pray for the lives and the well-being of the American hostages held in Iran. I cannot predict yet what will happen, but I hope you will join me in my constant prayer for their freedom."

Jimmy hoped that his defeat would serve as an impetus for the Iranians to release the hostages. The Americans agreed to release billions of dollars in Iranian assets frozen as a result of the hostage taking and the seizure of the embassy. Negotiations dragged on until the morning of January 20th, 1981. The hostages were all seated in an airplane and ready to depart but were held by orders of the Ayatollah, as a final act of personal spite towards Jimmy, until a few minutes after Ronald Reagan was sworn in as the 40th President of the United States. Jimmy was deeply wounded by this personally devastating loss. There was nothing left for him to do now except to go home... home to Plains.

Chapter XIII

BILLYGATE

"[No] matter what a waste one has made of one's life, it is ever possible to find some path to redemption, however partial." - Charles Frazier (Historical novelist.)

In the summer of 1978 Billy was asked to go to Libya on a good will tour. He thought that the trip, organized by Ahmed Shahati of Libya, was to help develop trade between the United States and Libya. At the time Libya was under the iron fisted control of a true enemy of the United States, the dictator Momar Kahdafi. When Jimmy heard that Billy was going to Libya, he forgot himself and cursed to high heaven. Nevertheless, Billy was soon on his way to the Middle East to begin a five day tour.

When he returned to the United States the press was all over him. While at a reception at the Waldorf Astoria Hotel in New York, he spoke to a journalist, saying that he thought we should develop a greater friendship towards Arabic nations. He was quoted as saying, "There are a lot more Arabs than Jews." As a result of this statement his image was marred, and requests for him to make public appearances suddenly dried up.

Not long after that incident, while waiting for a delegation from Libya to arrive at the airport, Billy decided to get out of his car that was parked by the runway and relieve himself. This crass event was reported in newspapers throughout the United States as Billy continued to make the most embarrassing headlines.

It was around this time, in 1979, that it became apparent to everyone, including Billy, that if he didn't do something about his drinking, and soon, he would completely self destruct. He was experiencing memory blackouts and could not hold down solid food. He vomited every time he tried to eat. He had not eaten for practically two months. His family and friends finally convinced him that he had to enter rehab.

His family doctor, Paul C. Broun, said, "I had been concerned for some time with Billy's drinking too much and smoking too much, but for the first time I could talk to him about it without him making a joke or ignoring it. He was sick and he was concerned, so he would talk about it seriously."

By the time he entered rehab he was consuming a half a gallon of vodka every single day. He stashed vodka in his suitcase in anticipation of the dry status of the hospital. When he was by himself the first night, he went to his bag only to find that it had been searched and his vodka taken away.

After three days without alcohol the insane torture began: sweating, shaking, vomiting and hallucinations without stop. He saw all manner of insects and even saw the devil himself sitting nearby and laughing at him. While suffering terribly from withdrawal for 11 long days, he would rather have been dead. Incredibly, once the dt's stopped the first thing he thought was that now that he was all clean he could start drinking fresh.

Soon, however, Billy began to recover and work on his rehabilitation. Jimmy arranged for Billy to enter a program at Long Beach Hospital in California. Jimmy used his power as commander-in-chief to reactivate Billy into the Marine Corps so that he would be eligible for admission to the military hospital. Even Sybil underwent three weeks of treatment to help her to appreciate the harm that came to her from living so long with an alcoholic and how she could help by "pulling away and letting Billy take responsibility for his own life." Over two months later he emerged from the hospital a sober man and would remain one for the rest of his life.

However, this didn't end his tendency to make poor decisions. Billy foolishly set himself up as an agent for Libyan crude oil coming into the United States. Further, he was given a loan of $220,000. from the Libyan government to help to facilitate sales. He had to register as a foreign agent in order to perform his duties, and the press began to call for investigations to connect Billy and Billygate, as the incident became known, to Jimmy.

Jimmy was livid. He and his staff already had their hands full and didn't wish to spend hours and hours on the Libyan scandal. But Jimmy would never personally attack his beloved and beleaguered brother.

Billy was given a chance to testify at length before a Senate committee and tell his side of the story. He had not been paid $220,000. by a government that was hostile to the United States for propaganda purposes but rather given a loan for legitimate business reasons, he explained. It was determined that Billy had not done anything illegal but had made serious errors in judgement.

Yet, allegations continued to fly. Reporters and politicians tried to tie Billy's errors to Jimmy or to members of his administration. There were suggestions that Billy had improperly used his influence concerning airplane sales to Libya. It was claimed that Jimmy attempted to obstruct the Justice Department investigation and had given Billy secret information about the case. There were even claims that Libyan money was paid to Jimmy.

There was no truth to any of these charges, but Jimmy and his staff had to waste precious time in an already very difficult election year trying to answer any and all questions. Jimmy prepared a report for the public and Congress explaining that he and his staff had nothing to hide and had nothing to do with Billy's foolish venture.

The Senate sub committee had reported that they found no evidence that Billy had influenced American policy. The report did say, however, that President Carter had been negligent in not dissociating himself from Billy's misadventure. This came one month before the crucial Democratic Convention.

The press would not let the issue die. Just before the convention it was reported that Jimmy had given secret cables to Billy regarding Libya to help in his business with them. But Jimmy had merely sent one unclassified document to Billy from the American Ambassador in Libya following Billy's visit in 1978. The document simply stated that Billy behaved himself and that the visit was positive.

As a result of the investigation Billy was unable to continue in any capacity with Libya and so had no job. In addition, he had spent all of his money and was now completely broke. He had become such an embarrassment that when the 1980 Democratic Convention came around he was invited not to attend by Jimmy's campaign staff.

Billy was undergoing a series of investigations by the federal government for his dealings with Libya and failure to pay taxes. He was under tremendous pressure, but when the 1980 election was over and Jimmy was defeated, the pressure was eased. He was quickly becoming irrelevant. Plains began to return to its sleepy ways and Billy was still out of work.

He foolishly had an affair with a woman in Atlanta, which nearly led to his divorce from Sybil. Generously, she forgave (but never forgot) his sin. The two worked out their problems and decided to stay together. He landed a job with a mobile home company, and he threw himself into the work with everything he had, work perhaps substituting for the distraction of alcohol.

His friends convinced him that he would be a great speaker to help others with serious alcohol problems. They thought that he would be able to readily relate to a lot of people that were like him. He started to give interviews and talk in public about his bout with alcohol. Sybil joined him, and the two talked to groups about the destructive nature of alcoholism.

At the end of his speeches, to his great delight and surprise, he always received a standing ovation. He thought that perhaps he had found a way to give back to people, to help them, and it appears that he did just that. He was no longer the clown; he was a good man who was making a difference in people's lives.

Now, all he needed, all he wanted, was a little time to make a real difference. He wanted to make it so that, in the end, his life will have mattered.

CHAPTER XIV

"MIZ LILLIAN, WHERE ARE YOU GOING NEXT?"

"Ah never knew you thought so much a me." Miz Lillian Carter (Registered Nurse, Peace Corps Volunteer, mother of a President of the United States.)

After she successfully completed her tour of duty in the Peace Corps, invitations began to pour in for Miz Lillian to speak. She was more than happy to oblige, and she began speaking every week to crowds, both large and small, about the Peace Corps and about the fact that old age did not have to prevent a person from having a full life. Before long she recorded over 650 such public appearances.

She readily embraced her role as a public speaker and made hundreds of campaign speeches on Jimmy's behalf when he ran for the Presidency. More often than not she was so comfortable that she made her presentation standing in bare feet. She personally enjoyed the experience but was also happy to be able to help.

It was always in her nature to be giving. Many years earlier, during the Great Depression, she would stand looking out of the front windows of the house in Archery and watch, with great pity in her heart, the darkly somber, unshaven faces of tramps as they stared, blankly, out from the countless open boxcars while the train slowly lumbered by.

They were men, mostly, beaten down by the complete devastation of a seemingly robust economy turned endless nightmare overnight. Often they traveled south in search of almost any form of employment or, perhaps, simply to escape the ravages of the freezing winters of the North.

And then there was the incessant parade of downtrodden men trudging along the red dirt road that passed in front of the Carter farmhouse. Some of these very men had been beaten, chased by dogs and otherwise mistreated for simply asking for food in exchange for an odd job or two at other nearby farms. Word spread among the tramps to avoid these places, but the opposite message was shared regarding the home of Miz Lillian.

When she was not off caring for the sick of the community, she would answer the knock at the back door and listen to the civil plea for something to eat and for a clean, cool drink of water. She would always provide a sandwich or some leftovers and a drink.

In addition, on occasion she was called upon to help in an emergency in town. For example, a boy, one day, climbed to the top of a water tank tower high above Plains. From his perch he proclaimed that he was going to kill himself. The townspeople pleaded with him to climb down, but he refused and said that he would leap the moment anyone climbed the ladder to try and rescue him. Eventually, Miz Lillian was sent for.

She instructed the others to back away and she began talking with the boy by shouting up and he shouting back down. He soon told her that his stepfather had been beating him and that he would rather die than continue living with the merciless beatings. After a while he felt comfortable enough with her to allow her to climb the ladder to talk to him side by side. She proceeded to scale the ladder and met the boy about one hundred feet up, the little town dizzyingly far below.

After talking for a while she called the sheriff forward and asked for his support in stopping the abuse. When he agreed, Miz Lillian also promised that they would all go together and speak to his stepfather. Convinced that his problem could be solved the boy agreed to come down. The three - the sheriff, the boy and Miz Lillian - went to the stepfather and helped to get him to understand that he had no choice but to stop hurting the boy.

As Jimmy grew more and more famous, word of Miz Lillian's exploits spread and she became an object of great curiosity to the people of America. It wasn't long before she was appearing on programs like the highly rated Tonight Show with Johnny Carson or Merv Griffin's popular talk show. She even did a cameo appearance on a made-for-TV movie starring the great comic Lucille Ball. Her endearing personality led to friendships with Carson and Griffin as well as saloon singer Dean Martin and even the legendary Frank Sinatra.

Reporters loved to question her because, more often than not, she fed them with something highly amusing to print. She didn't necessarily set out to amuse; she was just being herself. For example, she was asked if she would attend the ribbon cutting ceremony for Billy's beer business, and she answered: "Ah attended Jim-a's inauguration didn' Ah?"

Once she was asked, "Miz Lillian, aren't you proud of your son?" to which she responded, "Which one?" In addition, once when her offspring were involved in various national difficulties she was quoted as having said, "Sometimes, when Ah look at my children, Ah wish Ah had remained a virgin."

Once when asked what she was going to do for the weekend she said, "Ah'm goin home ta Plains this weekend because my dawg is in obedience school and his time is up. He's already smarter than Ah am."

After she met Pope Paul VI she told a reporter, "If Ah had my life ta live ovah again, Ah'd be a Catholic. Ah'm a Baptist, and they don't believe in havin' a drink late in the afternoon, o playin' poker-things Ah love ta do."

Capitalizing on her popularity Jimmy began asking her to help with some official events. When Israel's former Prime Minister Golda Meir died, he asked his mother to represent him as head of the delegation to the funeral. Following Marshall Josip Broz Tito of Yugoslavia's death, she joined Vice President Walter Mondale as a leader of the distinguished delegation to his funeral.

A reporter once asked, "Miz Lillian, where are you going next?" She said that she couldn't say because most of her assignments were to attend state funerals, and she couldn't predict who would be the next to die.

Then when President of India, Fakhruddin Ali Ahmed, died, Jimmy decided that she would be an excellent choice to head a large

American delegation to attend the funeral. Jimmy called her, "How would you like to go to India?" Miz Lillian said, "Ah'd love to go someday. Why?" Jimmy said, "How about this afternoon?" To which she quickly responded, "Okay, Ah'll be ready."

While in India she and the other delegates stopped to visit the village where she had served in the Peace Corps. Filled with apprehension and excitement, she envisioned kissing her old friends on the cheek and embracing the beautiful people she had given so much to and gotten so much from all those years ago.

When she arrived at the town there was no one there to greet her. Had they all forgotten her? Were all her efforts for nothing? Did she mean so little to them? She stood, chagrined, before the delegation. "Well, we can just walk down the street an roun' the corner, and Ah'll show y'all the apartment where Ah used ta stay."

Her head still in a dark and despairing cloud over her disappointment, she turned the corner and there she saw, silently waiting, more than ten thousand people. After a brief moment they exploded into applause and wild cheers.

When asked to speak she said, "Ah neva knew you thought so much a me. Ah'm so excited that Ah had forgotten tha Jimmy is president. Ah didn't even care. The first time Ah came here, Ah walked so much it seemed like a thousand miles, but Ah give you my word, Ah was happier walkin' here, sometimes barefoot, than Ah am now comin' in the President's plane."

CHAPTER XV

AN ACTIVIST IN THE FAMILY

"Every time a person sacrifices herself for a larger injustice, it aids in the cycle of change." Amy Carter (Political activist.)

In 1982, when she was 14, Amy returned to Washington to work as a Senate page for the summer. She was paid about $100. a week and was accompanied by Secret Service agents. She was furthering her education in mainstream American politics, but there was something else that attracted her more. She felt a need to express a more radical approach to solving America's and the world's problems.

In the mid-1980's Apartheid was still the law of the land in South Africa. Nelson Mandela remained behind bars, while black people were strictly separated from whites and kept in a sharply inferior position. Anti-Apartheid sentiment had spread to America and people, particularly the young, latched on to the cause and spoke out, organized boycotts and protested.

Amy, now a student at Brown University in Rhode Island, decided to join the effort and attended a demonstration at the South African embassy in Washington, DC. Outside, she joined other protesters in singing "We Shall Overcome." Amy then walked to the embassy door and tried to gain entrance, ostensibly so that she could express her opinion directly to the South African diplomats. She was refused entry, and instead of moving on as instructed by the police, she steadfastly remained. It wasn't long before she was handcuffed and taken away.

Reporters wanted to know how her parents, especially Jimmy, felt about her actions. She told them, "When Ah decided to do it this morning, Ah called home and they said it was 'O.K.'. He said, 'Ah am proud to be my daughter's father.'"

Amy joined other young people of the era in trying to recapture the radical/activist attitude that was so prevalent in the 1960's. She said that Brown and other schools are "loosening up, getting back into the old spirit" of protest. Amy was also concerned with U.S. policy in Central America, particularly in Nicaragua where the Reagan administration and, later, the Bush, Sr. administration, supported the efforts of the Contras to overthrow the leftist government of the Sandinistas.

She typically wore a green army surplus-style coat with a T-shirt and other casual clothing, a far cry from the carefully attired first daughter. Amy was living in a cooperative with 15 other vegetarian students not too far from the campus of Brown University.

Her father had met with success and with failure by using traditional means to achieve political goals. In the end his plans were cut short, and he had to step down. Amy thought that more radical measures would help to get things done. She had developed an extremely empathetic heart and a strong sense of justice.

Along with one hundred Brown University students, she occupied the school's administration building for two hours to protest the over

$35 million portfolio the school had invested in companies that did business with South Africa.

Amy was arrested along with fourteen other college students at a local office of International Business Machines. The police arrested the students after about thirty minutes of a sit in at the IBM office. The student protestors wanted the company to stop doing business with South Africa.

Soon Amy found herself protesting with the best of them. A major '60's radical, Abbie Hoffman, joined her and about sixty other students at an anti-CIA recruitment protest at the University of Amherst in Massachusetts. Amy, Hoffman, and fifty eight others were arrested for various charges including trespassing, disorderly conduct, and obstructing justice.

Abbie Hoffman was a co-founder and essential member of the radical Youth International Party (Yippie) movement in the late 60's and early 70's. He was most famous for being a member of the Chicago Seven group that were charged with conspiracy and inciting a riot during the 1968 Democratic National Convention in Chicago.

Abbie was arrested in 1973 on charges related to his intention to sell cocaine. Although he always maintained that he was framed, he jumped bail and went into hiding. He turned himself in 1980 and received a one year sentence for which he served four months. He returned to political activism and worked closely with Amy in the Amherst protest.

Amy was arrested at Amherst when, after coming out of a school building, she observed the police presence and thought that the force was beyond reasonable. She later said, "There were, Ah would say, 60 or 80 cops in riot gear, billy clubs, mace, with four or five police dogs - it was really terrible." She said the police unnecessarily beat a protester, and that's when she decided to be arrested again. She was charged with disorderly conduct and trespassing.

Although she faced the possibility of time behind bars, she pushed for a jury trial rather than negotiate a dismissal of the case or a very small punishment, because she wanted to "spotlight the CIA. Ah haven't really been thinking about the jail part. Ah've just been thinking about the trial itself. Whatever happens, Ah'm sure Ah can handle it." She was glad to have the story get a lot of publicity, but, "Ah really don't like it when there's a political action involving many students, and there's a story written about me, and not the action."

Her lawyer was Leonard I. Weinglass, who had defended Hoffman and other members of the Chicago Seven in 1968. The defense relied on what is known as the necessity doctrine, affirming that the protesters were violating a law to prevent a greater wrong. Amy said, "If we win, it would mean the jury has decided the C.I.A. is guilty of larger crimes than what we committed." She did not deny that she blocked a road outside one of the University's halls in support of those who were sitting in.

Amy had climbed up a fire escape and through a window into the college administration building and later sat down to block a bus carrying arrested protesters because she thought that it would help end illegal activities in Central America by the Central Intelligence

Agency. When she testified, she explained her actions by saying, "Every time a person sacrifices themselves for a larger injustice, it aids in the cycle of change."

The judge allowed testimony on the CIA activities in Central America. The defendants characterized the case as "The CIA on trial." When the judge and jury left the court for a lunch break, the assembled audience gave Amy a standing ovation. Political activists of the 60's era, Daniel Ellsberg and Ramsey Clark, also testified. Amy said, "My parents told me they were proud of me. They said they were surprised we had accomplished this much and gotten this far."

Amy, Abbie and 13 other protesters were found not guilty. Upon hearing the verdict Jimmy said he was a "very proud father tonight. Amy's been arrested four times, three times for protesting apartheid and this last time for what she considers, and Ah consider, illegal activity of the CIA in Nicaragua."

Later, Amy was put on limited probation by a Brown University disciplinary board for her participation in a campus protest on South Africa's apartheid policy. Amy and 20 other students were said to have taken part in an action that "disrupts or materially interferes with the rights of others." They were charged with having disturbed a meeting of the University Corporation to demand that the school sell its stock in companies with ties to South Africa.

In the summer Amy was dismissed from Brown for failing to keep up her course work. Apparently her political actions were a major distraction from her academic responsibilities. That winter, Amy said that she would not return to Brown, insisting that she wasn't expelled but that she just wanted to attend a southern school.

Amy went on to graduate from Tulane University in New Orleans with a master's degree in fine arts and art history. It appears that by this point she had gotten her fervent need for radical political activism out of her system.

Chapter XVI

A SECOND CHANCE

"I think of a hero as someone who understands the degree of responsibility that comes with his freedom." - Bob Dylan (Musician, songwriter, singer and poet.)

It is December, 2002.

Jimmy sits on a stage in the Grand ballroom of the Oslo City Hall in Norway and listens as Georgia-born soprano Jessye Norman sings; "He's got the woods and the waters in his hands...He's got the birds and the bees right in his hands...He's got the whole world in his hands." When she concludes her song Jimmy blows her a kiss.

Then Gunnar Berge, Norwegian Noble Committee Chairman steps up to the lectern in the center of the stage and speaks; "Now I call upon the Noble Peace Prize winner of 2002, Jimmy Carter, to give his Noble lecture, please." Jimmy rises and walks to the lectern. He is receiving the prize, as his award citation cites in part, because

(his) mediation was a vital contribution to the Camp David Accords between Israel and Egypt, in itself a great enough achievement to qualify for the Noble Peace Prize. At a time when the cold war between East and West was still predominant, he placed renewed emphasis on the place of human rights in international politics.

Through his Carter Center...he (sic) has...undertaken very extensive and persevering conflict resolution on several continents. He has

shown outstanding commitment to human rights, and has served as an observer at countless elections all over the world.
He has worked hard on many fronts to fight tropical diseases and to bring about growth and progress in developing countries.

Jimmy is enjoying this wonderful moment of great recognition for his valiant efforts in the cause of world peace, particularly since he so unhappily left the White House more than twenty years earlier.

When he had returned to Plains after his devastating defeat he was welcomed home with great hoopla by the whole community. A few days later he was asked by President Reagan to travel to Germany to welcome the newly released hostages. After that mission was completed and Jimmy returned to the home that he and Rosalynn had owned since 1961, the only home he ever owned, in Plains, he lay down upon his bed and closed his eyes.

The darkness offered a soothing respite from the far too complicated world. Now, at long last, he could rest. The hostages were all safely on their way home and all the other cares and burdens of the presidency were completely off of his shoulders. It grew darker and for just a brief minute he was walking barefoot on the hot Georgia clay with A.D. on his way to the secret fishing hole. Then ever so slowly a black velvet curtain began to drop before his eyes and then melt and drip down like thick chocolate syrup over the scene and he was in a profound sleep, perhaps the deepest he had ever known.

When he opened his eyes, at last, he looked at the clock and the time was the same as when he closed them. He had slept for twenty four hours. Now it was time to face a life he did not wish for, a life in which he had absolutely no idea what was in store for him. Perhaps more disappointment, perhaps more loss, perhaps...emptiness.

To make matters worse, it wasn't long before Jimmy learned about the state of his finances. He and Rosalynn were deeply in debt. The warehouse had consistently lost money, and Jimmy realized that there was nothing left to do but to sell the business.

The two had neglected their home for the last decade during which they were either in the Governor's mansion, on the campaign trail, or in the White House. Now that they were back with time on their hands and no firm direction, they threw themselves into the labor of repairing and improving their home. They did the demanding manual labor themselves, finding it cathartic as they tried to figure out what would be their next step.

Soon Jimmy began to study the thousands of pages of notes he had so assiduously kept during his four years on Pennsylvania Avenue. He began to put his memoirs together even before he had a publisher. He was anxious to get everything straight in his own mind.

In addition, he offered his services to Emory University in Atlanta. There he was named a distinguished professor and taught in all of the different schools of the university. His classes ranged from a small group to an auditorium filled with scores of students.

Jimmy and Rosalynn soon began to plan his Presidential library and raise the many millions needed to complete the project. Jimmy was certain that one thing he did not want was a monument to himself.

Even though he was busy spending time with friends, planning the library, teaching and writing there was still something missing. Where was the real purpose to his life? Where was the contribution to the world? What if he were to live for decades more, after all he was only 56. What lasting impact can he have on the betterment of the world?

Then one night it came to him. The Carter Center! Rosalynn was asleep, then turned over and opened her eyes to see Jimmy sitting straight up in the bed. She asked, "Wha's the matah Jim-a? Are you ill? Did you have a nightmare?" It was later written that he responded,

> I know what we can do at the library. We can develop a place to help people who want to resolve disputes. There is no place like that now. If two countries really want to work something out, they don't want to go to the United Nations and get one hundred and fifty other countries involved in the argument. I know how difficult it is for them to approach each other publicly, and they take a chance on being embarrassed by a rebuff from the other party. We could get good mediators that both sides would trust, and they could meet with no publicity, no fanfare, perhaps at times in total secrecy. If there had been such a place, I wouldn't have had to take Begin and Sadat to Camp David. There've been a lot of new theories on conflict resolution developed since that time, too, and we might put some of them into use.

Soon, he and his assistant, Dr. Steve Hochman, set up the first office on the top floor of the Emory University Library. They defined their mission as one that would not only deal with conflict resolution but also such pressing topics as global health, the environment, human rights, and nuclear arms control.

Within a couple of years both the library and the Carter Center opened. It wasn't long before Jimmy and representatives from the Center were traveling all around the world observing scores of elections and helping to strengthen democracies.

One special issue that the Carter Center has taken on is the effort to completely eradicate Guinea worm disease. The disease, in which a worm travels downward through the human body, is incredibly painful and is accompanied by fever, nausea and vomiting. It can also result in arthritis and paralysis.

When the Center first began to address the issue there were 3.5 million cases in over 20 countries in Asia and Africa. The Center trained thousands of village volunteers to help health workers in managing the disease as well as reporting cases and treating patients. Because of these efforts it is estimated that the disease has been reduced by 99.99% and it is believed that millions of cases have, thus far, been averted.

One important mission that Jimmy undertook on behalf of the Center concerned Haiti. In 1994 President Bill Clinton asked him to try to negotiate the peaceful departure of some of Haiti's military leaders so that the duly elected President Jean-Bertrande Aristide could return from exile to his rightful position of power. Clinton was on the verge of leading a coalition invasion of the Island country. In fact, thousands of heavily armed troops were on their way as Carter, at the last minute, successfully negotiated the departure of the military leaders and thereby avoided a bloodbath and provided for the peaceful return of Aristide.

When he isn't advancing the many causes of the Carter Center Jimmy makes time to write. He enjoys considerable success as an author, having written nearly thirty books that, for the most part, have been well-received. His first, after leaving the White House, was his story of his years in the Oval Office, *Keeping Faith: Memoirs of a President*. He also tackled the subject of the Middle East in *The Blood of Abraham*, and talked about his early run for political office in *Turning Point: A Candidate, a State, and a Nation Come of Age*.

In 2001 he produced an excellent memoir of his early life in Archery and Plains, *An Hour Before Daylight: Memories of a Rural Boyhood*. As though to demonstrate his verbal creativity, he wrote *Always a Reckoning, and Other Poems*. He went on to write *The Virtues of Aging*, a volume that stirred little controversy. His book, on the contrary, *Palestine Peace Not Apartheid*, has been the recipient of both bouquets and brickbats. Though he attempted to be objective in his call for a revitalization of the peace process between Palestine and Israel, some concluded that he favored the former at the expense of the latter. He also wrote about the discrimination and violence against girls and women in *A Call to Action: Women, Religion, Violence and Power* in 2014.

Jimmy and Rosalynn became active in Habitat for Humanity. This organization "brings people together to build homes, communities and hope." They volunteer every year to help build homes and to raise awareness for affordable housing.

When Jimmy was interviewed by Barbara Walters in the 1990's she asked, "Mr. President, looking back on your time as a submarine officer, a farmer and businessman, as governor, and in Washington, what has been the best of all?" He responded, "By far, my best years are those Ah'm enjoying right now, since Rosalynn and Ah left the White House."

When he gave his lecture in Oslo at the ceremony in which he was honored with the Nobel Peace Prize he touched on what he saw as the most serious of the greatest challenges that the world faced;

> ...the growing chasm between the richest and poorest people on earth. Citizens of the ten wealthiest countries are now seventy-five times richer than those who live in the ten poorest ones, and the separation is increasing every year, not only between nations but also within them. The results of this disparity are root causes of most of the world's unresolved problems, including starvation, illiteracy, environmental degradation, violent conflict, and unnecessary illnesses that range from Guinea worm to HIV/AIDS.
>
> War may sometimes be a necessary evil. But no matter how necessary, it is always an evil, never a good. We will not learn how to live together in peace by killing each other's children. The bond of our common humanity is stronger than the divisiveness of our fears and prejudices. God gives us the capacity for choice. We can choose to alleviate suffering. We can choose to work together for peace. We can make these changes - and we must.

AFTERWORD

"Life has no meaning. Each of us has meaning and we bring it to life. It is a waste to be asking the question when you are the answer." - Joseph Campbell (Mythologist, writer and lecturer.)

Plains High School teacher Miss Julia Coleman died in 1973 at the age of 84. She was honored in 1977 when Jimmy quoted her in his inaugural address and again in 2002 in his speech in which he accepted the Nobel Peace Prize.

Jimmy's much admired Uncle Tom Gordy, was stationed in Guam and was captured in the first month of World War II. He was then transported to Japan. In the summer of 1943 he was officially pronounced dead. His wife began to receive a widow's pension and she and her children moved to San Francisco where she remarried about a year later.

When the war ended Uncle Tom was found to be alive; beaten and, half-starved, he weighed less than 100 pounds. When he returned home he tried to reconnect with his wife, but it didn't work out. He met and married another woman and completed his career in the Navy, then opened a tavern. He died in 1975.

Anwar al-Sadat won the Nobel Peace Prize as a result of the treaty he signed with Israel. In 1981, while reviewing a parade in Cairo, Sadat was assassinated in part because of the peace treaty.

In the early 1980's Miz Lillian was diagnosed with breast cancer and temporarily went into remission. Then in 1983 her daughter Ruth died of pancreatic cancer at the age of 54. The following month, October, Miz Lillian died at the age of 85. She was laid to rest next to Mr. Earl.

A nursing center in Plains was named in her honor. Emory University established the Lillian Carter Center for International Nursing in memory of the work she did in India. The Atlanta Regional Office of the Peace Corps has named an award in her honor for volunteers over 50 who make the biggest contribution.

Jack Clark did not live to see Jimmy achieve the Presidency, having died while Jimmy was in the service, but Rachel did. She died in 1986 at the age of 96.

Sadly, after years of heavy smoking, and with an apparent genetic predisposition towards it, Billy Carter developed pancreatic cancer. Jimmy tried to help by getting Billy into an experimental cancer treatment program. He did enter the program but to no avail. His weight dropped from 180 pounds to a mere 125.

He spent much of his remaining days with his youngest son, planting flowers and behaving with decency toward his loved ones and friends. Within a year he was dead. He was only 51 years old. His last words were to his ever faithful wife, "Ah love you, Sybil." She was there from the beginning and through all the wild days of his celebrity, through his drunkenness, scandal and redemption, and she was there at the very end.

Billy is buried at Lebanon Cemetery just a mile outside of Plains near his beloved daddy Earl, Miz Lillian, and a number of the other Carter ancestors. By many of those across America who remember him, he is thought of as nothing more than a joke and a buffoon, and the very mention of his name can often evoke laughter. But he was a complicated and intelligent man whose fight against his demons got the better of him. In the end he had triumphed over his battle with alcohol, not having a drop to drink for years, but he was marked to be a tragic figure. That was his destiny and it was fulfilled.

Admiral Rickover, the "father of the nuclear navy", died at the age of 86. Jimmy spoke at his mentor's funeral.

Abbie Hoffman died at the age of 52 in 1989. Long a sufferer of severe bi-polar disorder, he decided to commit suicide.

In 1980 Ayatollah Khomeini and Iran became involved in an intense war with neighboring Iraq. The war lasted until 1988 and resulted in the death of hundreds of thousands of people. Khomeini died on June 3, 1989, at the age of 86.

In 1990 Jimmy's sister Gloria, an avid motorcyclist, died of Pancreatic cancer at the age of 63. All three of Jimmy's siblings and his father died from the same disease. In 1977 Gloria had collected the letters her mother sent from India while serving in the Peace Corps and formed a book, "Away From Home: Letters to My Family."

Menachem Begin also won the Nobel Peace Prize for his work at Camp David. He died following a heart attack in 1992. Begin has been considered to be among the greatest Israeli's of all time by the Israeli people.

Colonel Charlie Beckwith died suddenly at the age of 65 in 1994. In commenting on his mission to Iran he had said, "It was the biggest failure of my life. I cried for the eight men we lost. I'll carry that load on my shoulders for the rest of my life."

Byron De La Beckwith managed to avoid conviction for Medgar Evers' murder until 1994 when, attitudes towards race having changed significantly in the South, justice finally caught up with him and he was sentenced to life imprisonment. He died in a hospital bed a few miles from his prison home in 2001 at the age of 80.

Lester Maddox ran unsuccessfully for governor and for president. He never repented for his racist ways. He died, at the age of 87, in 2003 of cancer.

Ronald Reagan successfully completed two terms as President during which he helped to bring an end to the Cold War. After having been diagnosed with Alzheimer's disease he died on June 5, 2004.

Gerald Ford went on to enjoy a long and fruitful retirement after leaving the White House in 1977. Ford died in 2006 at the age of 93 years and 165 days, the longest life of any American President, outliving Ronald Reagan by 45 days. Over the years Gerry and Jimmy had developed what has been declared the most intensely personal friendship between any two presidents in history. Jimmy delivered a eulogy at Ford's funeral in response to his wishes.

Ted Kennedy never tried for the presidency again. He spent the rest of his life in the Senate where he and his staff authored more than 300 bills that were enacted into law. He was known as "The Lion of the Senate" because of his tenacity. Although clearly liberal he was not afraid to work with Republicans to reach compromises. He championed the cause of universal health care. In 2008 he was diagnosed with a malignant brain tumor. He died in 2009 and rests in Arlington Cemetery near the graves of his brothers, Jack and Bobby.

The daughter of the gardener, Madhavi Vinod, that Miz Lillian taught to read and write grew up to earn a doctorate and to become president of a University in India.

Mary Fitzpatrick eventually received a full pardon from the State of Georgia. She is still employed by the Carter family today.

A.D. Davis served four years in prison having been convicted of forgery. He married, had twelve children, and after his release from the penitentiary worked in a sawmill and lived out a quiet life in Plains.

In the early 1990's Amy was in New Orleans spending her summer working in a bookstore that was managed by a young man named James Wentzel. It wasn't long before the two got to know each other and eventually became engaged. Their wedding took place at the Pond House on September 1, 1996. The ceremony was a quiet affair attended by a few friends and relatives. Amy wore a 1920's hand embroidered dress and walked down a path that she lined with magnolia flowers. Ever the non-conformist she refused to have her father give her away because "she did not belong to anyone." She kept her maiden name.

The couple first went to New Orleans and then later on they moved to Atlanta where they bought a house not far from the Carter Center. In 1999 they had a son, Hugo James Wentzl.

Today, she serves on the board of the Carter Center. She illustrated two of her father's books. Amy now lives a quiet, private life.

Jimmy and Rosalynn's three sons, Jack, Chip and Jeff, all married and live successful lives. Jack's son Jason, served in the Peace Corps, then married. Jason and his wife, Katie, produced Jimmy's and Rosalynn's first great-grandchild, Henry Lewis Carter. In 2014 Jason ran for Governor of Georgia.

Epilogue

FINISHING STRONG

"Do not go gentle into that good night. Old age should burn and rage at close of day. Rage, rage against the dying of the light." - Dylan Thomas (Poet.)

It is a recent Sunday.

A number of people have been waiting in line, with serene patience, some for over one hour, outside of the Maranatha Baptist Church. It is a pleasant simple brick structure with four columns in the front and a pedestal pitched roof above, then a tall elegant spire topped by a white cross. The people either stand silently or they speak in friendly, hushed tones to an equally reserved neighbor or two. One woman can be overheard to say, "I've seen him before and I said to myself, 'If ever I'm in Plains I'll be sure to go see him once more'." The morning is clear, calm and surprisingly cool for August in Georgia.

Large white double-doors swing open and three Secret Service agents, all looking very much the same in their dark suits, stride out and swiftly set up a table and a metal detector. Instantaneously, a feeling of excitement and great anticipation spreads through the gathering.

An agent signals with his hand and the first in line obediently marches forward, robotically empties his pockets on the table, walks through the metal detector, has the contents of his pockets returned to him and, relieved to have made it through uneventfully, happily enters the Church. One by one the people are checked and the churches wooden pews quickly fill from front to back and ultimately to the capacity of about 300.

It is an unadorned place obviously designed with simplicity in mind. The floor is covered by a green rug and there are purple and light green stained glass windows and an oversized vase filled with fresh flowers in the middle in front of an altar. Carnations, daises and sunflowers are on prominent display. A bare wooden cross hangs on the front wall.

In a small private room behind the altar Jimmy and Rosalynn wait for the go ahead from the agent in charge. Jimmy's hair is all white now, his face deeply lined with wear and wisdom after the experience of nine full decades. He has donned a dark checkered sports jacket, his reading glasses are in his left breast pocket, a small microphone is attached to his lapel, a bolo tie loosely hangs around his neck. He wears grey pants, brown loafers and a white shirt covering a light weight bulletproof vest. He looks to be, and is, very cool as he turns to his wife and smiles gently.

Now the agent nods his head and Jimmy and Rosalynn walk through the door and without fanfare are seen by the joyous congregation. The agent takes a seat, quite rigidly, in a chair on the front left, Rosalynn sits, demurely, in a pew to the side and Jimmy steps with confidence to the front and center, faces the congregation and begins to speak in his assertive, clipped yet friendly manner.

He is carrying on a tradition that his father had started so many years before; that of teaching a Bible class. Any Sunday that he is in Plains you can find him here speaking about the lessons of the "good book". He is as mentally sharp now as he was when he was a much younger man first running for political office.

Archery is nothing more than a long walk away and its influences weigh heavily inside of Jimmy. He speaks to the assemblage but it is not just him talking, it is also Rachel Clark and Daddy and Julia Coleman and many others.

He pauses for a moment, looks up and gazes down the center aisle, and he can see the white doors swing open and outward, a shaft of silver and white light swiftly floods the room. There, out in front, are the red brick steps and beyond that the deep green grass and high, high above in a clear blue sky the Georgia sun shines like a dazzling orange ball.

Works Consulted

Amdur, Richard. *World Leaders Past and Present: Menachem Begin.* New York, N.Y.: Chelsea House Publishers, 1988.

Andrus, Cecil. Telephone interview. June 2008.

Aufderheide, Patricia. *World Leaders Past and Present: Anwar Sadat.* New York, N.Y.: Chelsea House Publishers, 1985.

Bourne, Peter G. *Jimmy Carter: A Comprehensive Biography from Plains to Post presidency.* New York, N.Y.: Scribner, 1997.

Brinkley, Douglas. *The Unfinished Presidency.* New York, N.Y.: Penguin Putnam Inc., 1998.

Camp David. Lawrence Wright. Dir. Molly Smith. With Richard Thomas, Hallie Foote, Khaled Nabawy, Ron Rifkin, 2014.

Carroll, Raymond. *Anwar Sadat.* New York, N.Y.: Franklin Watts, 1982.

Carter, Billy and Sybil with Ken Estes. *Billy.* Newport, R.I.: Edgehill Publications, 1989.

Carter, Hugh with Leighton, Frances Spatz. *Cousin Beedie and Cousin Hot: My Life with the Carter Family of Plains, Georgia.* Englewood Cliffs, N.J.: Prentice-Hall, 1978.

Carter, Jimmy. *An Hour Before Daylight; Memories of a Rural Boyhood.* New York, N.Y.: Simon and Schuster Paperbacks, 2001.

---. *An Outdoor Journal: Adventures and Reflections.* Fayetteville, N.C.: University of Arkansas Press, 1994.

---. *The Nobel Peace Prize Lecture.* New York, N.Y.: Simon and Schuster, 2002.

---. *Keeping Faith: Memoirs of a President.* New York, N.Y.: Bantam Books, 1982.

---. *Sharing Good Times.* New York, N.Y.: Simon and Schuster, 2004.

---. *Why Not the Best.* Fayetteville, N.C.: University of Arkansas Press, 1996.

---. *A Remarkable Mother.* New York, N.Y.: Simon and Schuster, 2008.

---. *Turning Point: A Candidate, A State and A Nation Come of Age.* New York, N.Y.: Three Rivers Press, 1992.

---. *Christmas in Plains: Memories.* New York, N.Y.: Simon and Schuster, 2001.

---. *Beyond the White House: Waging Peace, Fighting Disease, Building Hope.* New York, N.Y.: Simon and Schuster, 2007.

---. *Palestine Peace Not Apartheid.* New York, N.Y.: Simon and Schuster, 2006.

---. *A Call to Action: Women, Religion, Violence and Power.* New York, N.Y.: Simon and Schuster, 2014.

---. *Always a Reckoning and Other Poems.* New York, N.Y.: Crown Publishers, 1995.

---. *The Virtues of Aging.* New York, N.Y.: Random House Publishing Group, 1998.

---. *The Blood of Abraham: Insights Into the Middle East.* Fayetteville, AR.: University of Arkansas Press, 2007.

Carter, Lillian and Spann, Gloria Carter. *Away From Home; Letters to My Family.* New York, N.Y.: Simon and Schuster, 1977.

Carter, Rosalynn. *First Lady From Plains.* Boston, MA.: Houghton Mifflin Company, 1984.

Carter, William 'Buddy'. *Billy Carter: A Journey Through the Shadows.* Marietta, GA.: Longstreet, Inc., 1999.

Connelly, Joel and Andrus, Cecil. *Politics Western Style.* Seattle, WA.: Sasquatch Books, 1998.

Glad, Betty. *Jimmy Carter: In Search of the Great White House.* New York, N.Y.: W.W. Norton and Company, 1980.

The Green Hand. Georgia Agricultural Education Curriculum Office. Athens, GA.: 1940.

History of Plains. Americus, GA.: Gammage Print Shop, 1976.

Hochman, Steve. Personal interview. Aug. 2008.

Haugabook, Allene. Personal interview. Aug. 2008.

Jewish Virtual Library. The American/Jewish Cooperative Enterprise. Military Casualties in Arab/Israel Wars.

Jimmy Carter: Adult Bible Class. Maranatha Baptist Church. Plains, GA: Feb. and Aug. 2008.

Jimmy Carter: American Experience. Dir. Adriana Bosch. WGBH Educational Foundation, 2002.

Jimmy Carter: Man From Plains. Dir. Jonathan Demme. With Jimmy Carter, Rosalynn Carter, Lillian Carter, Elizabeth Hayes. Armian Pictures, 2007.

Jimmy Carter: The President From Plains. SpeechWorks, 2007.

Kennedy, Edward M. *True Compass.* New York, N.Y.: Grand Central Publishing, 2006.

New American Bible. Catholic Book Publishing Corporation, 1992.

The New York Times. *Spoiled or Not, Amy Carter, 8, Is Village Darling in Plains, GA.,* June 22, 1976.

---. *Amy Carter Will go to a Public School Near the White House,* Nov. 29, 1976.

---. *Amy Carter's Nurse is Accepted by Church,* Mar. 21, 1977.

---. *Amy Carter to Accept Elephant,* Apr. 1, 1977.

---. *Amy Carter Revises Vision of Chainsaws,* Dec. 11, 1977.

---. *Helen Hayes and Amy Carter Share Stage at the White House,* Dec. 15, 1977.

---. *Billy Carter in Spotlight Anxiety on Libyan Connection,* Aug. 3, 1980.

---. *Billy Carter's Brother's Mess,* Aug. 6, 1980.

---. *Amy Carter Arrested,* Apr. 9, 1985.

---. *Amy Carter, Abbie Hoffman Held in Protest,* Nov. 26, 1986.

---. *Amy Carter, Abbie Hoffman Tell Strategy,* Jan. 8, 1987.

---. *Trial Opens for Amy Carter and 14 Over a Protest,* Apr. 10, 1987.

---. *Amy Carter tells Court She Sat in Road to Alter CIA Policy,* Apr. 14, 1987.

---. *Amy Carter is Acquitted Over Protest,* Apr. 16, 1987.

---. *Amy Carter is Reported Dismissed From College,* July 20, 1987.

---. *Billy Carter Dies of Cancer at 51,* Sept. 26,1988.

---. *Abbie Hoffman, 60's Icon, Dies; Yippie Movement Founder was 52,* Apr. 14, 1989.

Plains Historical Preservation Trust. *History of Plains, Georgia.* Fernandina Beach, FL.: Wolfe Publishing, 2003.

Rifkin, Jeremy and Howard, Ted. *Redneck Power: The Wit and Wisdom of Billy Carter.* New York, N.Y.: Bantam Books, 1977.

Stapleton, Ruth Carter. *Brother Billy.* New York, N.Y.: Harper and Row, Publishers Inc., 1978.

Sunday Mornings in Plains. Bible Study with Jimmy Carter. *Leading a Worthy Life.* New York, N.Y.: Audioworks, Simon and Schuster, 2007.

---. *Measuring Our Success.* New York, N.Y.: Audioworks, Simon and Schuster, 2007.

---. *Bringing Peace to a Changing World.* New York, N.Y.: Audioworks, Simon and Schuster, 2007.

Tanner, Laura. Personal interview. Aug. 2008.

Thompson, Hunter S. *Jimmy Carter and the Great Leap of Faith.* Rolling Stone, June 3, 1976.

Walters, C.L. Personal interview. Aug. 2008.

Wead, Doug. *All the President's Children.* New York, N.Y.: Atria Books, 2003.

Williams, Jan. Personal interview. Aug. 2008.

Photo Credits

Author's Collection

Jimmy Carter National Historic Site

Jimmy Carter Presidential Library and Museum

The United States National Archives and Records Administration

ABOUT THE AUTHOR

The author with The President and Mrs. Carter in Plains, Georgia

Michael Spencer Hayes has a Master's Degree in American History and has taught U.S. History as an Adjunct Professor at the State University of New York. He has contributed to the Long Island Historical Journal and Modern American Environmentalists, a biographical encyclopedia. He is the author of Oak Hill: Voices from an American Hamlet, an Oral History. Currently Mike is a teacher in the Social Studies Department in East Meadow High School. He lives in Manhattan.

Printed in the United States
By Bookmasters